305.80

WOKE RACISM

WOKE
RACISM

■ ■ ■

*How a New Religion Has
Betrayed Black America*

JOHN McWHORTER

PORTFOLIO / PENGUIN

Portfolio / Penguin
An imprint of Penguin Random House LLC
penguinrandomhouse.com

Most Portfolio books are available at a discount when purchased in quantity for
sales promotions or corporate use. Special editions, which include personalized
covers, excerpts, and corporate imprints, can be created when purchased in
large quantities. For more information, please call (212) 572-2232 or e-mail
specialmarkets@penguinrandomhouse.com. Your local bookstore can also assist
with discounted bulk purchases using the Penguin Random House corporate
Business-to-Business program. For assistance in locating a participating
retailer, e-mail B2B@penguinrandomhouse.com.

The Prologue and Chapters 1 and 2 have been previously published in different
form in the author's Substack newsletter, "It Bears Mentioning" (2021).

Library of Congress Cataloging-in-Publication Data
Names: McWhorter, John H., author.
Title: Woke racism : how a new religion has betrayed
Black America / John McWhorter.
Description: [New York] : Portfolio/Penguin, [2021] |
Includes bibliographical references and index.
Identifiers: LCCN 2021024506 (print) | LCCN 2021024507 (ebook) |
ISBN 9780593423066 (hardcover) | ISBN 9780593423073 (ebook)
Subjects: LCSH: African Americans—Social conditions—1975- |
Anti-racism—United States. | Race discrimination—United States. |
Whites—United States—Attitudes. | Critical race theory—United States. |
United States—Race relations.
Classification: LCC E185.86 .M4273 2021 (print) |
LCC E185.86 (ebook) | DDC 305.800973—dc23
LC record available at https://lccn.loc.gov/2021024506
LC ebook record available at https://lccn.loc.gov/2021024507

Printed in the United States of America
4th Printing

BOOK DESIGN BY ELLEN CIPRIANO

This book is dedicated to each who find it within themselves to take a stand against this detour in humanity's intellectual, cultural, and moral development.

CONTENTS

PREFACE

I 'M NOT ONE FOR long introductions. However, before we begin I would like to give the reader a sense of the lay of the land.

This book is not a call for people of a certain ideology to open up to the value of an open market of ideas, to understand the value of robust discussion, and to see the folly of defenestrating people for disagreeing with them. My assumption is that the people in question are largely unreachable by arguments of that kind.

Rather, this book is a call for the rest of us to understand that people of a certain ideology are attempting to transform this country on the basis of racism. They do not know it and, when apprised of it, cannot admit it. But the rest of us must.

My main aims will be:

1. To argue that this new ideology is actually a religion in all but name, and that this explains why something so

destructive and incoherent is so attractive to so many good people.

2. To explain why so many black people are attracted to a religion that treats us as simpletons.

3. To show that this religion is actively harmful to black people despite being intended as unprecedentedly "anti-racist."

4. To show that a pragmatic, effective, liberal, and even Democratic-friendly agenda for rescuing black America need not be founded on the tenets of this new religion.

5. To suggest ways to lessen the grip of this new religion on our public culture.

I hope my observations will serve as one of many contributions to our debate over what constitutes "social justice." My aim is not to merely pen a screed to stoke the flames among people who already agree with me. I want to reach those on the fence, guilted into attention by these ideologues' passion and rhetoric but unable to disregard their true inner compass. I want them to commit with confidence to what I seek: helping make things better for real people.

What this book is not.

We need not wonder what the basic objections to this book will be. I mischaracterize and/or disrespect religion. I am oversimplifying. The real problem is the militarized right wing. I'm not black enough to write this book. I'm not nice, and so on. I will get all of that out of the way as we go on, and then offer some genuine solutions. But first, what this book is not:

1. This book is not an argument against protest. I am not arguing against the basic premises of Black Lives Matter, although I have had my differences with some of its offshoot developments. I am not arguing that the Civil Rights movement of the 1950s and '60s would have been better off sticking to quiet negotiations. I am not arguing against the left. I am arguing against a particular strain of the left that has come to exert a grievous amount of influence over American institutions, to the point that we are beginning to accept as normal the kinds of language, policies, and actions that Orwell wrote of as fiction.

2. I am not writing this book thinking of right-wing America as my audience. People of that world are welcome to listen in. But I write this book to two segments of the American populace. Both are what I consider to

be my people, which is what worries me so much about what is going on.

One is *New York Times*–reading, National Public Radio–listening people who have innocently fallen under the impression that pious, unempirical virtue signaling about race is a form of moral enlightenment and political activism, and ever teeter upon becoming card-carrying unintentional racists themselves. In this book I will often refer to these people as "white," but they can be of any color, including mine. I am of this world. I read *The New Yorker*, I have two children, I saw *Sideways*. I loved both *The Wire* and *Parks and Recreation*.

The other is black people who have innocently fallen under the misimpression that for us only, cries of weakness constitute a kind of strength, and that for us only, what makes us interesting, what makes us matter, is a curated persona as eternally victimized souls, ever carrying and defined by the memories and injuries of our people across the four centuries behind us, ever "unrecognized," ever "misunderstood," ever in assorted senses unpaid.

3. This is not merely a book of complaint. My goal is not to venture a misty statement that today's hyper-wokesters need to understand that a diversity of opinions is crucial to a healthy society. Citing John Stuart Mill at them

serves no purpose; our current conversations waste massive amounts of energy by missing the futility of "dialogue" with them. Of one hundred fundamentalist Christians, how many do you suppose could be convinced via argument to become atheists? There is no reason that the number of people who can be talked out of this religion should be any higher.

As such, our concern must be how to continue with genuine progress in spite of this ideology. How do we work around it? How do we insulate people with good ideas from the influence of liturgical concerns? How do we hold them off from influencing the education of our young people any more than they already have? How do we conduct socially gracious existences amid the necessity of engaging with their religious doctrine, presented with Cotton Mather's earnestness and impregnable insistence, when almost none of them will actually understand that they are making religious rather than secular arguments?

That is, my interest is not "How do we get through to these people?" We cannot, at least not enough of them to matter. The question is "How can we live graciously among them?" We seek genuine change in the real world, but for the duration we will have to do so while ever encountering bearers of a gospel itching to smoke out heretics and ready on a moment's notice to tar us as moral perverts.

I write this viscerally driven by the fact that the ideology in question is one under which white people calling themselves our saviors make black people look like the dumbest, weakest, most self-indulgent human beings in the history of our species, and teach black people to revel in that status and cherish it as making us special. I am especially dismayed at the idea of this indoctrination infecting my daughters' sense of self. I can't always be with them, and this anti-*humanist* ideology may seep into their school curriculum. I shudder at the thought: teachers with eyes shining at the prospect of showing their antiracism by filling my daughters' heads with performance art instructing them that they are poster children rather than individuals. Ta-Nehisi Coates, in *Between the World and Me*, wanted to teach his son that America is set against him; I want to teach my kids the reality of their lives in the twenty-first, rather than the early to mid-twentieth, century. Lord forbid my daughters internalize a pathetic—yes, absolutely pathetic in all of the resonances of that word—sense that what makes them interesting is what other people think of them, or don't.

Many will nevertheless see me as traitorous in writing this book as a black person. They will not understand that I see myself as serving my race by writing it. One of the grimmest tragedies of how this perversion of sociopolitics makes us think (or not think) is that it will bar more than a few black readers from understanding that this book is calling for them to be treated with true dignity. However, they and everyone else should also know: *I know quite well that white readers will be more likely to hear out views like this when they are written by a black person, and I consider it nothing less than my duty as a black person to write this book.*

A version of this book written by a white writer would be blithely dismissed as racist. I will be dismissed instead as self-hating by a certain crowd. But frankly, they won't really mean it, and anyone who gets through the book will see that whatever traits I harbor, hating myself or being ashamed of being black is not one of them. And we shall move on.

WOKE RACISM

1

WHAT KIND OF PEOPLE?

A S I WRITE THIS in the summer of 2020, Alison Roman, a food writer for *The New York Times*, is on suspension. You might wonder just what a food writer could do to end up temporarily dismissed by her employer. Roman's sin: In an interview, she passingly criticized two people for commercialism, model and food writer Chrissy Teigen and lifestyle coach Marie Kondo. Roman was Twitter-mobbed for having the nerve, as a white woman, to criticize two women of color.

Teigen is half white and half Thai. Kondo is a Japanese citizen. Neither of them are what we typically think of as people of color in the sense of historically conditioned and structurally preserved disadvantage. However, in 2020, the mere fact of a white person criticizing not just one but two (apparently the plurality tipped the scales) non-white persons justified being shamed on social media and disallowed from doing her work. Roman, as a white person, was supposedly punching down—i.e., "down" at two people very wealthy, very successful, and vastly better known than her. Her whiteness trumped all, we were told.

Roman, now typical of such cases, ate crow with an apologetic statement about how she had reflected and realized her error. Teigen even said that she did not think Roman deserved to be sanctioned. But no matter—a kind of fury, passed off as being "antiracist," now has a supreme power in our public moral evaluations, and this required that Roman be pilloried in the town square. Her Wikipedia entry will forever include a notice that she was deemed a racist, billboard style, despite that most Americans likely see that she did nothing that remotely deserved such treatment, and despite that she would not have been treated that way as recently as a few years ago. She later left the *Times* permanently.

What kind of people do these things? Why do they get away with it? And are we going to let them continue to?

THE SAME YEAR, Leslie Neal-Boylan lasted only a few months as dean of nursing at the University of Massachusetts Lowell. The problem was that in the wake of statements nationwide after the murder by police officers of George Floyd, Dean Neal-Boylan had the audacity to pen this blinkered, bigoted screed to her colleagues and staff:

I am writing to express my concern and condemnation of the recent (and past) acts of violence against people of color. Recent events recall a tragic history of racism and bias that continue to thrive in this country. I despair for our future as a nation if we do not stand up against violence against anyone. BLACK LIVES MATTER, but also, EVERYONE'S LIFE MATTERS. No one should have to live in fear that they will be targeted for how they look or what they believe.

A certain crowd decided to read Neal-Boylan as chiming in with those who resist the slogan "Black Lives Matter" by answering that "All Lives Matter," as if BLM is somehow claiming that black lives matter *more*. However, one could read Neal-Boylan as meaning this only via not reading well. She started out by lamenting "a tragic history of racism and bias," and no, she didn't mean that it existed only in the past and that black people need to get over it, because she also wrote that the racism and bias "continue to thrive in this country."

However, because her composition included the three words "everyone's life matters," she was reported to her superiors and quickly out of a job without even being allowed to defend herself. Why was Leslie Neal-Boylan's email deemed a missive from someone unfit to supervise people dedicated to healing and giving comfort? A child would wonder why—as would a time traveler from as recently as 2015. But Neal-Boylan's detractors were deemed authoritative.

What kind of people do these things? Why do they get away with it? And are we going to let them continue to?

. . .

Also in the same year, 2020, David Shor, a data analyst at a progressive consulting firm, lost his job. He had tweeted a study by a black Ivy League political science professor, Omar Wasow, showing that violent black protests during the long, hot summers of the late 1960s were more likely than nonviolent ones to make local voters vote Republican. Shor's intent was not to praise this, but to disseminate the facts themselves as a glum announcement—one that had been covered eagerly by liberal media shortly before this.

Certain parties on Twitter, though, didn't like a white man tweeting something that could be taken as criticizing black protest in the wake of George Floyd's murder. The consulting firm took heed and expelled Shor.

What kind of people do these things? Why do they get away with it? And are we going to let them continue to?

What kind of people do these things?

All of these cases occurred because of the influence of a frame of mind we could term Third Wave Antiracism, a movement whose adherents are more often termed "social justice warriors" or "the woke mob."

One can divide antiracism into three waves along the lines that feminism has been. First Wave Antiracism battled slavery and legalized segregation. Second Wave Antiracism, in the 1970s and '80s, battled racist attitudes and taught America that being racist is a moral flaw. Third Wave Antiracism, becoming mainstream in the 2010s, teaches that because racism is baked into the structure of society, whites' "complicity" in living within it constitutes racism itself, while for black people, grappling with the racism surrounding them is the totality of experience and must condition exquisite sensitivity toward them, including a suspension of standards of achievement and conduct.

Under this paradigm, all deemed insufficiently aware of this sense of *existing while white* as eternal culpability require bitter condemnation and ostracization, to an obsessive, abstract degree that leaves most observers working to make real sense of it, makes people left of center wonder just when and why they started being classified as backward, and leaves millions of innocent people scared to pieces of winding up in the sights of a zealous brand of inquisition that seems to hover over almost any statement, ambition, or achievement in modern society.

So one might ask why I seem to consider it such an issue that some food columnist, some nursing school dean, and some data analyst have had their lives derailed by this movement. But I write not of something happening to a few unlucky people, but operating within the warp and woof of society. No one can know just when or how Third Wave Antiracist proselytizing may blindside them while they are going about their business.

It is losing innocent people their jobs. It is coloring academic inquiry, detouring it, and sometimes strangling it like kudzu. It forces us to render a great deal of our public discussion of urgent issues in double-talk any ten-year-old can see through. It forces us to start teaching our actual ten-year-olds, in order to hold them off from spoiling the show in that way, to believe in sophistry in the name of enlightenment. On that note, Third Wave Antiracism guru Ibram X. Kendi has written a book on how to raise antiracist children, called *Antiracist Baby*. (You couldn't write it better—are we in a Christopher Guest movie?) This and so much else is a sign that Third Wave Antiracism forces us to pretend that performance art is politics. It forces us to spend endless amounts of time listening to nonsense presented as wisdom, and pretend to like it.

Graduate students and professors write me and my podcast sparring partner, economist Glenn Loury, in droves, frightened that this new ideology will ruin their careers, departments, or fields, as they also do to other organizations, often on private email accounts to avoid being smoked out by anyone at the institutions they work for. People in positions of influence are regularly being chased from their posts because of claims and petitions that they are insufficiently antiracist. School boards across the country are forcing teachers and administrators to waste time on "antiracist" infusions into their curricula that make no more sense than anything proposed under China's Cultural Revolution. Did you know that objectivity, being on time, and the written word are "white" things? Did you know that if that seems off to you, then you are one with George Wallace, Bull Connor, and David Duke?

As recently as 2008, Christian Lander wrote with wry humor in *Stuff White People Like* of "being offended" as something a certain kind of "white" person enjoys doing, alongside their film festivals and vintage T-shirts. Just over a dozen years later, one reads that chapter with a shudder that the kind of person Lander was referring to will see it over your shoulder and launch into a hissing tirade about how there is nothing funny about people trying to dismantle the prevalence of white supremacy and all whites' "complicitness" in it. If he were to write that book today, Lander would be unlikely to include that joke, which is an indication of the extent to which there is something in the air that we hadn't seen until quite recently. A critical mass of the people he was referring to no longer just quietly pride themselves on their enlightenment in knowing to be offended about certain things, but now see it as a duty to excoriate and shun those (including black people) who don't share their degree of offense.

To some, all of that may sound like mere matters of manner and texture. But Third Wave Antiracism also outright harms black people in the name of its guiding impulses. Third Wave Antiracism insists that it is "racist" for black boys to be overrepresented among those suspended or expelled from schools for violence, which, when translated into policy, is documented as having led to violence persisting in the schools and lowered students' grades. Third Wave Antiracism insists that it is "racist" that black kids are underrepresented in New York City schools requiring high performance on a standardized test for admittance, and demands that we eliminate the test rather than direct black students to resources (many of them free) for practicing the test and reinstate gifted programs that shunted good numbers of black students into those very schools just a generation ago. That the result will be a lower quality of education in the schools, and black students who are less prepared for exercising the mind muscle required by the test taking they will encounter later, is considered beside the point.

Third Wave Antiracism, in its laser focus on an oversimplified sense of what racism is and what one does about it, is content to harm black people in the name of what we can only term dogma.

For example, the Third Wave Antiracist is deeply moved by a collection of tenets that, stated clearly and placed in simple oppositions, translate into nothing whatsoever:

1. When black people say you have insulted them, apologize with profound sincerity and guilt.	Don't put black people in a position where you expect them to forgive you. They have dealt with too much to be expected to.
2. Don't assume that all, or even most, black people like hip-hop, are good dancers, and so on. Black people are a conglomeration of disparate individuals. "Black culture" is code for "pathological, primitive ghetto people."	Don't expect black people to assimilate to "white" social norms, because black people have a culture of their own.
3. Silence about racism is violence.	Elevate the voices of the oppressed over your own.
4. You must strive eternally to understand the experiences of black people.	You can never understand what it is to be black, and if you think you do you're a racist.

5. Show interest in multiculturalism.	Do not culturally appropriate. What is not your culture is not for you, and you may not try it or do it.
6. Support black people in creating their own spaces and stay out of them.	Seek to have black friends. If you don't have any, you're a racist. And if you claim any, they'd better be *good* friends—albeit occupying their private spaces that you aren't allowed in.
7. When whites move away from black neighborhoods, it's white flight.	When whites move into black neighborhoods, it's gentrification, even when they pay black residents generously for their houses.
8. If you're white and date only white people, you're a racist.	If you're white and date a black person, you are, if only deep down, exotifying an "other."
9. Black people cannot be held accountable for everything every black person does.	All whites must acknowledge their personal complicitness in the perfidy of "whiteness" throughout history.
10. Black students must be admitted to schools via adjusted grade and test-score standards to ensure a representative number of them and foster a diversity of views in classrooms.	It is racist to assume a black student was admitted to a school via racial preferences, and racist to expect them to represent the "diverse" view in classroom discussions.

I suspect that, deep down, most know that none of this Catechism of Contradictions makes any sense. Less obvious is that it was not even composed with logic in mind.

The idea is to strike a happy medium between the poles? But there's no way that the people promulgating this "race thing" litany would ever allow that anyone had. One way we know it is that over several decades the promulgators never have. Another way we know it is more straightforward: There simply is no logical "medium" to be found between these alternates. One could not perform any pair of them simultaneously.

Why do so many wise people elevate these tenets as wisdom? The reason simply cannot be logic, because there is none to be had. The reason is because these tenets serve a purpose other than the one they are purported to serve.

Namely, each component by itself serves to condemn whites as racist. To apologize shows your racism; to be refused the apology, too, shows your racism. To not be interested in black culture shows your racism; to get into black culture and decide that you, too, want to rap or wear dreadlocks also shows your racism. The revelation of racism is, itself and alone, the point, the intention, of this curriculum. As such, the fact that if you think a little, the tenets cancel one another out is considered trivial. That they serve their true purpose of revealing people as bigots is paramount—sacrosanct, as it were.

Or, as it *is*. Specifically, these tenets serve the purpose of expressing the central pole, the guiding watchcry, of Third Wave Antiracist religion. It is rarely stated explicitly, but decisively steers its adherents' perspective on existence and morality.

Third Wave Antiracism's needlepoint homily par excellence would be the following:

> Battling power relations and their discriminatory effects must be the central focus of all human endeavor, be it intellectual, moral, civic, or artistic. Those who resist this focus, or even evidence insufficient adherence to it, must be sharply condemned, deprived of influence, and ostracized.

It can seem an oddly particular perspective, this rigid focus on battling differentials in power. Power is rampantly abused and creates endless suffering, to be sure. An enlightened society must be always addressing this and trying to change it. However, given the millions of other things that constitute human life and endeavor, to impose that undoing power differentials must *center all possible endeavor in what we call life* is a radical proposition.

I began encountering this worldview early in my academic career, and it took me a long time to perceive that various conflicts I have encountered in my work on linguistics (as well as race) have been variations on the same problem. The humanities and social sciences in academia have long harbored many people who see their discipline's goal as to Fight the Power. I recall my first taste of it, when a graduate student gave a guest lecture on *My Fair Lady*, in which she noted that Higgins talks more than Eliza and therefore wields power over the narrative. *Who's talking?* she taught us to ask. This perspective is certainly correct, but a part of me couldn't quite wrap my head around her general implication that to savor *My Fair Lady*'s music or wit is to be taken in, that an enlightened person looks down on the piece as the story of a lower-class female's self-expression brutally suppressed by a bullying oldish man of letters.

But back then, this kind of analysis was a minority view. Alarmist journalism depicted college campuses as being overrun by "tenured radicals," but this was a cartoon. At the time, that kind of ideology was one of many dishes one sampled at the university buffet. The problem is that today, this reductive, prosecutorial, and ultimately joyless kind of thinking actually is taking over not just university culture but American culture at large.

In any case, one of the main power differentials in our society is the one conditioned by racism. It is this Salem-style religious commitment to "battling" it that made the excommunications of Alison Roman, Leslie Neal-Boylan, and David Shor make sense to so many perfectly sane people.

Of course, the "race thing" Catechism of Contradictions makes no sense, but then neither does the Bible. To the Third Wave Antiracist, the sense our society must make above all other kinds is tarring whites as racist and showing that you know that they are racist. Any cognitive dissonance this occasions is "not what we need to be talking about," because antiracism is everything—*regardless of logic*.

Why do they get away with it?

Third Wave Antiracism's claims and demands, from a distance, seem like an eccentric performance from people wishing they hadn't missed the late 1960s, dismayed that so much of the basic work is done already. Seeking the same righteous fury and heartwarming sense of purpose and belonging, their exaggerations and even mendacities become inevitable, because actual circumstances simply do not justify the attitudes and strategies of 1967.

In an alternate universe, these people would be about as important as the Yippies were back in the day, with marijuana on their "flag," applying to levitate the Pentagon and smacking pies in people's faces. They were a fringe movement good for a peek, and occasionally heightened awareness a tad. But they were unimportant in the grand scheme of things, and justifiably so. What makes the difference is that today's Third Wave Antiracists have a particular weapon in their arsenal that lends them outsized power, much more impactful than a cream pie.

Ironically, the weapon is so lethal because of the genuine and invaluable change that has occurred in our sociopolitical fabric over the past decades. That change is that to the modern American, being called a racist is all but equivalent to being called a pedophile. A lot of very important people fought to make it that way, and few of us would wish they had not. But the problem is that the Third Wave Antiracists now piggyback on it. A key part of their tool kit is that they call those who disagree with them racists, or the more potent term of art of our moment, "white supremacists." That kind of charge has a way of sticking. To deny it is to confirm it, we are taught; once the charge is hurled, it's like you're caught in a giant squid's tentacles. At least you can wash a cream pie off.

We need not suppose Third Wave Antiracists do this cynically to amass power. Take a look at, or listen to, that family member, neighbor, or co-worker you know who thinks this way and ask yourself whether they really give any indication of being a power seeker. The Third Wave Antiracist genuinely reviles racism, as do most of us. They also seek a great deal else in the name of this that seems hopelessly impractical, idealist, or just plain mean. But under our current conditions, the shakiness of their platform does not get in their way. This is because they can at any time shout out that you are a racist—and they do.

And to all but a very few, being called a racist is so intolerable today that one would rather tolerate some cognitive dissonance and fold up. This wouldn't have worked as well in, say, 1967. In that America, many white people called racists by this kind of person, for better or for worse, would have just taken a sip of their cocktail and said, "I don't think so at all." Or even just "Fuck you!" Today—because of progress, ironically—things are different. Now most cringe hopelessly at the prospect of being outed as a bigot, and thus: In being ever ready to call you a racist in the public square, the Third Wave Antiracist outguns you on the basis of this one weapon alone. Even if their overall philosophy is hardly the scriptural perfection they insist it is, that one thing they can and will do in its defense leaves us quivering wrecks. And thus they win.

The people wielding this ideology and watching its influence spread ever more are under the genuine impression that they are forging progress, that reason and morality are in flower. However, society is changing not because of a burgeoning degree of consensus in moral sophistication. What is happening is much cruder. Society is changing not out of consensus, but out of fear—the fear of the child cowering under the threat of a smack from an angry parent, the serf cowering under the threat of a disfiguring smash from the knout. The statements of solidarity from seemingly every institutional entity, the social media selfies of people "doing the work" of reading *White Fragility*, anyone pretending to entertain notions that the hard sciences need to "open up" to "diverse" perspectives by pulling back from requiring close reasoning—all of this is a product of not enlightenment, but simple terror. We have become a nation of smart people attesting that they "get it" while peeing themselves.

Unbeautiful but real. Third Wave Antiracism exploits modern Americans' fear of being thought racist to promulgate not just antiracism, but an obsessive, self-involved, totalitarian, and utterly unnecessary kind of cultural reprogramming. One could be excused for thinking this queer, glowering kabuki is a continuation of the Civil Rights efforts of yore, the only kind of new antiracism there could be. Its adherents, now situated in the most prestigious and influential institutions in the land, preach with such contemptuous indignation that on their good days they can seem awfully "correct."

Are we going to
let them continue to?

The question is: Will we knuckle under to this and pay-to-play? Or will we assert that these people are gruesomely close to Hitler's

racial notions in their conception of an alien, blood-deep malev-
olent "whiteness," in their simplistic conception of what it means
to be "black," in their crude us-versus-them conception of how
society works, as if we were all still rival bands of australopith-
ecines?

MANY REVIEWS WILL DISMISS this book as being about something that doesn't really matter. But if that's true, why are you
reading it? You are reading it because this religion has started to
drive you crazy and you want to know what the hell this is and
what to do about it.

You get First Wave Antiracism and think of segregation as
an ancient barbarity.

You're right.

You get Second Wave Antiracism—i.e., roughly equivalent
to what Gloria Steinem and Betty Friedan did for feminism—
and think we should all work to truly see black people as equal
to whites and deserving of all that whites get.

You're right.

You see Third Wave antiracism telling you that you are
morally bound to conceive of ordinary statements that once
were thought of as progressive, like "I don't see color," as racist.
That if you are white you are to despise yourself as tainted permanently by "white privilege" in everything you do. That you
must accept even claims of racism from black people that make
no real sense, or, if you are black, must pretend that such claims
are sacrosanct because the essence of your life is oppression.

Whatever color you are, in the name of acknowledging "power," you are to divide people into racial classes, in exactly the way that First and Second Wave antiracism taught you not to, including watching your kids and grandkids taught the same, despite that progress on racism has been so resplendent over the past fifty years that an old-school segregationist brought alive to walk through modern America *even in the deepest South would find it hard not to turn to the side of the road and retch at what he saw.*

You don't get it. *You are right again.*

You wonder what in God this new thing is that you are expected to bow down to at the PTA meeting, or when you open up websites of what were once your favorite news sources, or when you listen to callers on National Public Radio, or when you submit to "diversity training" at work that leads to nothing you can perceive except the mouthing of vacuous mantras, or when you stay quiet when somebody at a jolly gathering with you and your kids casually roasts as today's fifth-grade outcast some writer you actually have always agreed with and you decide to stay silent.

All of that nags like an eyelash caught behind your contact lens. They insist that self-mortification is political activism—*fail.* They insist that being black is ever and only oppression from the white man—*fail.* That black people labor under threat of the return of disenfranchisement as a people because Republicans try to depress black turnout to lower Democrat tallies, even though black women were central in determining the election of Joe Biden as president along with a black American vice president? *Fail.* Yet if you venture any genuine pushback, you are tarred on social media as a racist.

You, black or not, are not crazy to get that this glowering double-talk doesn't wash. And your job is to learn to cover your ears against what feels like verbal jiujitsu from those whose sense of significance is founded in denying reason and teaching people who have already been through enough to build their identities around a studied sense of victimhood.

Of course, they say they are pursuing "social justice," thus telling the rest of us that we are resisting social justice. Don't get tripped up. They are using the term to refer to their very specific and questionable sense of what social justice is, and as such, to ask us whether we are "against social justice" qualifies as a dirty trick along the lines of being asked if you still beat your spouse.

WE WILL NEED A CRISPER label for these problematic folk. I will not title them "social justice warriors." That and other labels such as "the woke mob" are unsuitably dismissive. One of the key insights I hope to get across in this book is that most of these people are not zealots. They are mostly thoroughly nice people. They are your neighbor, your friend, possibly even your offspring. They are friendly school principals, people who work quietly in publishing, lawyer pals. Heavy readers, good cooks, musicians. It's just that, sadly, what they become, solely on this narrow but impactful range of issues, is inquisitors.

I considered titling them the Inquisitors. But that, too, is mean. I'm not interested in mean; I want to get around these people so we can actually move ahead. But I intended it as an accurate metaphor—this ideology directly impedes getting ahead.

Author and essayist Joseph Bottum has found the proper term, and I will adopt it here: We will term these people the Elect. They do think of themselves as bearers of a wisdom, granted them for any number of reasons—empathic leaning, life experience, maybe even intelligence. But they see themselves as having been chosen, as it were, by one or some of these factors, as understanding something most do not. "The Elect" is also good in implying a certain smugness, which, sadly, is an accurate depiction. Then too, it challenges the people in question to consider whether they really think of themselves as superior in this way. Of course, most of them will resist the charge. But with it sitting in the air, in its irony, they may feel moved to resist the definition, which over time may condition at least some of them to temper the excesses of the philosophy—just as after the 1980s many started disidentifying from being "too PC."

But most importantly, terming these people the Elect implies a certain air of the past, à la *The Da Vinci Code*. This is apt, in that the view they think of as, indeed, sacrosanct is directly equivalent to views people centuries before us were as fervently devoted to as today's Elect are. The medieval Catholic passionately defended persecuting Jews and Muslims for reasons we now understand were rooted in lesser facets of being human. We spontaneously "other" those antique inquisitors in our times, but right here and now we are faced with people who harbor the exact same brand of mission, just against different persons.

In 1500 it was about not being Christian. In 2020 it's about not being *sufficiently* antiracist, with adherents supposing that this is a more intellectually and morally advanced cause than antipathy to someone for being Catholic, Jewish, or Muslim. They do not see that they, too, are persecuting people for not adhering to their religion.

Grammar lessons in how we will use this term:

We are confused and hurt by *the Elect*.

The person who threatens us is *an Elect*.

We must learn to glean when someone is *Elect*. Is he *Elect*?

Did he say something *Elect*? Take heed, and if he says more *Elect* things, disengage.

He went all *Elect* on me.

They were up on some *Elect* shit.

Electism manifests itself in degrees, of course. There are especially abusive Elect ideologues. Some are comfortable ripping into people in person; others largely restrict the nastiness to social media. Still other Elect do not go in for being actively mean but are still comfortable with the imperatives, have founded their sociopolitical perspectives firmly upon them, and are hard-pressed to feel comfortable interacting socially with people in disagreement. They allow the openly abusive Elect to operate freely, seeing their conduct as a perhaps necessary unpleasantness in the goal of general enlightenment.

In this book, I do not wish to imply that the Elect are all of the especially abusive type; the vast majority are not. It is a frame of mind compatible with all variations of human temperament, not a fanaticism. Fundamentalists hope their Good News reaches the whole world someday, but they encompass all personality types, as do all Christians, Muslims, and Baha'is. Thus we must not imagine that the Elect is prototypically a picketing shouter. Just as plausibly, they are an easy-mannered sort with some kids and a quiet grin, who you would never imagine subscribing to something extremist, unempirical, and tribalist. They may well even play the ukulele while singing Odetta songs and sipping Knob Creek. Yet this selfsame person will, with no hesitation, sign a letter requesting the firing or public shaming of someone who has contravened the Elect's doctrine.

Thus, in working with the Elect, we must not be on the alert for hotheads. The challenge of the Elect is precisely that they are no more pushy, arrogant, or otherwise socially un-schooled than anyone else—they are just folks. The problem is the degree to which the more hostile adherents have come to influence, robustly, so very many less argumentative but equally devout others, whose increasing numbers and intimidating buzz-words have the effect of silencing those who see Elect philoso-phy as flawed but aren't up for being mauled. The Elect are, in all of their diversity, sucking all of the air out of the room. It must stop.

We will hear that this is a book "against antiracism," and thus racist (cue the fist bumps). But as most of us can see, there is a difference between being antiracist and being antiracist in a hostile way, where one is to pillory people for what, as recently as ten years ago, would have been thought of as petty torts or even as nothing at all, to espouse policies that hurt black people as long as supporting them makes you seem aware that racism exists, and to pretend that America never makes any real progress on racism and privately almost hope that it doesn't, because it would deprive you of a sense of purpose. We must conceive of such people as adherents of a sect called the Elect.

And more to the point:

> *What kind of people do these things?* Religious fundamentalists.
> *Why do they get away with it?* Because they scare us in calling us heretics in the public square.
> *Are we going to let them continue to?* Not if we want to keep our intellectual, moral, and artistic culture from being strangled by what is not a sociopolitical program but a religion. The Elect are operating on the basis of a new religion emerging before us here in our own times. The next chapter will expand on this point.

Do not heed those who say that this religion isn't important. Make no mistake: These people are coming after your kids.

2

THE NEW RELIGION

S OMETHING MUST BE UNDERSTOOD: I do not mean
that these people's ideology is "like" a religion. I seek no
rhetorical snap in the comparison. I mean that it actually is a
religion. An anthropologist would see no difference in type
between Pentecostalism and this new form of antiracism. Language is always imprecise, and thus we have traditionally re-
stricted the word *religion* to certain ideologies founded in creation
myths, guided by ancient texts, and requiring that one subscribe
to certain beliefs beyond the reach of empirical experience. This,
however, is an accident, just as it is that we call tomatoes vegetables rather than fruits. If we rolled the tape again, the word *religion* could easily apply as well to more recently emerged ways of
thinking within which there is no explicit requirement to subscribe to unempirical beliefs, even if the school of thought does
reveal itself to entail such beliefs upon analysis. One of them is
this extremist version of antiracism today.

With the rise of Third Wave Antiracism we are witnessing

the birth of a new religion, just as Romans witnessed the birth of Christianity. The way to get past seeing the Elect as merely "crazy" is to understand that they are a religion. To see them this way is not to wallow in derision, but to genuinely grasp what they are.

One thing that will discourage a general perception of them in this way is that they themselves will resist the charge so heartily. This is understandable. Early Christians did not think of themselves as "a religion," either. They thought of themselves as bearers of truth, in contrast to all other belief systems, whatever they chose to call themselves. In addition, in our times, it will feel unwelcome to the Elect to be deemed a religion, because they do not bill themselves as such and often associate devout religiosity with backwardness. It also implies that they are not thinking for themselves.

However understandable their objections, though, we must not let them distract us as we roll up our sleeves and fashion a way of living among people devoted permanently to this new, yes, religion. Their resistance will miss the larger picture, which is less about the Elect as individuals than about how we make sense of a way of thinking they share, one that seems so obsessive and hurtful from the outside. To make sense of it, we must understand them—partly out of compassion and partly in order to keep them from destroying our own lives. This can happen only if we process them not as crazed, but as parishioners.

To do this, we must examine the ways in which their new religion so closely parallels older ones. It makes what can seem like a mess of weird opinions and attitudes into something quite coherent.

The Elect have superstition.

It is inherent to a religion that, amid various other tenets and commitments, one is to accept certain suspensions of disbelief.

Certain questions are not to be asked or, if asked, only politely. The answer one gets, despite being somewhat half-cocked, is to be accepted. The Christian is allowed to ask why the Bible is so self-contradictory, or why God allows such terrible things to happen. But no one has had a smackdown answer for two millennia anyway, and what's key is that you believe.

One internalizes an etiquette that it stops there. One is to classify the issues as "deep." A way to fashion this as of a piece with rational thought is to assume that the relevant questions "always lead to more questions."

Elect philosophy requires the same standpoint. One is not to ask "Why are black people so upset about one white cop killing a black man when black men are at much more danger of being killed by one another?" Or one might go ahead and ask, only to receive flabby answers after which further questions are unwelcome. A common answer is that black communities do protest black-on-black violence. But anyone knows that the outrage against white cops is much, much vaster. All of 2020 after March was about outrage against white cops. None of

2020 was about black communities aggrieved at their sons and nephews and cousins killing one another, a trend that spiked in poor black neighborhoods nationwide in the summer of 2020, as it had in countless summers before.

Is there a real answer? You will hear that black men are killing one another within a racist "structure." But as an intelligent person, you know that doesn't answer the question. An elegant way of putting this is that there's a difference between being killed by a fellow citizen and being killed by a figure of state authority. But does that mean "It's not as bad if we do it to ourselves"?

We get no real answer at that point except rolled eyes. One is simply not to question, and people can be quite explicit about it. For example, in "the conversation" about race that we are so often told we need to have, the tacit idea is that black people will express their grievances and whites will agree. "Oh, no, no—you're caricaturing," the Elect object when we characterize their conversations that way, but they are unable to specify a single thing they might learn in said conversation, as opposed to what we heathen (see below) might. Rather, just as the Christian may be told that the main thing is to believe, the Elect are taught that the main thing is to not be racist, regardless of the implications of their beliefs for the people they are supposedly fighting for.

Or we are told that a major reason for adjusting standards for university admissions is to foster diversity so that "diverse" students can contribute their perspectives in the classroom. But then "diverse" students regularly say that they hate being responsible for representing the "diverse" view in the classroom.

The Elect's response? To chalk up that expectation of participation as in itself "racism"—despite that this *undercuts a prime justification for racial preferences.* Question this closely and you just don't "get it." Rather, we might just accept this as questions always leading to more questions—and, after a certain point, stop asking them.

What you actually don't "get" in your quest to wring logic out of incoherent positions like these is that for the Elect, battling racism is to be questioned only in ways that reinforce the idea that the Elect are correct—*even at the cost of basic sense.* This is superstition. We scoff at this reductive mindset when reading of the Bolsheviks and Stalin a century ago in black-and-white photos, but we cringingly allow it as a new paradigm when it's on the behalf of black people in America last week on YouTube.

This is all very Abrahamic, as religion goes. *Muslim, Islam*— the core of such words in Arabic is the consonants *s-l-m*, which constitute the concept of submission. One submits not only to a God. To suspend disbelief is a kind of submission. It is no accident that many of the white Elect spontaneously put their hands above their heads as an indication that they understand that they bear "white privilege." Think of this type, asserting "Oh, I know I'm privileged!" while holding their hand up, palm out, like a Pentecostal. Maybe they think they are being a little "hip" and taking a page from black gestures—but then upon reflection they would surely condemn that as "cultural appropriation" of a kind they surely revile. They are so comfortable with that gesture in attesting to their privilege because of an overriding impulse: to indicate submission to a power up there looking down on them.

Or even this: When Elect white people at protests started taking a knee for extended periods to indicate general wokeness after George Floyd's murder, it was a submission to Elect imperatives. Superstition is often observed through ritual gestures such as throwing salt over one's shoulder for good luck—or postures of prayer.

The Elect have clergy.

A useful illustration of this clergy is something that never completely made sense in 2014. To wit, why was Ta-Nehisi Coates's essay "The Case for Reparations" received so *very* rapturously?

Yes, it was well written, but aesthetics was not why people were tweeting about this magazine article in actual tears. Something larger had to be afoot, especially given that reparations for slavery had been endlessly discussed in the media just fifteen years before, including in a hit book, Randall Robinson's *The Debt*. It was read ardently nationwide, just as Coates's essay was. If social media and Kindle had existed in the early 2000s, *The Debt* would still be read widely today. But from the way Coates's article was received, one might have supposed that it was the first time reparations had been presented to the American public.

Or at least that it was the most convincing case ever made for reparations. But it would be hard to say that Coates's case outstripped Robinson's (or many others) in any suasional way, especially since Robinson's case was a whole book. Plus, Coates (like Robinson) gave no real specifics as to just how reparations might work. The issue is not whether Coates wrote a good essay. He did, and then some. But its reception as another *Unsafe at Any Speed* or *Silent Spring* was, in itself, a puzzle.

Here is what solves that puzzle: People loved Coates's article not as politics. Quite simply, almost no one thinks reparations are actually going to happen *in a way that would leave its advocates actually satisfied*. "The Case for Reparations" was received, rather, as a sermon. In that, it was a good one. But its audience was seeking proclamation, not information. Yes, some readers, especially younger ones, were encountering the reparations argument for the first time. But most reading people were not. Plenty of people singing of the article as if it were a newly discovered Dead Sea Scroll had more than a few gray hairs. They knew the drill already.

In this, although Coates hardly intended it, for his fans he has been not just a teacher but a preacher. A. O. Scott perfectly demonstrated this clerical role in our discourse when he called Coates's book *Between the World and Me* "essential, like water or air." That the American intelligentsia embraced that quote so snugly was an indication in itself, in that Scott's encomium sounds as if it refers to the Greatest Story Ever Told.

To approach this kind of communication as information sharing is to miss its essence. Few receive what these thinkers are saying as new. Think of the preacher praised for his sermon as people file out of church. It probably wasn't the kind of sermon that, for most of those people, blew their minds. They enjoyed it because it was a beautiful rendition of that which they knew before, and it gave them comfort.

On race, the Elect cherish certain top-rate thinkers for their gifts in phrasing, repeating, and crafting artful variations upon points considered crucial. These are their priests, their clergy. You need your preacher to keep telling the religion's truth, and to tell it often, since the superstitious, nonempirical wing of the ideology is easy to drift away from as real life impinges ever upon you in daily existence.

Whites flock and even pay to listen to Robin DiAngelo teach them the counterintuitive lesson that they are racist cogs in a racist machine, with societal change possible only when they admit this and shed their racism (which will make poor black people less poor how and when, exactly?). In this, because what she is teaching is religious thought, she is a traveling celebrity preacher in the vein of Aimee Semple McPherson. The Center for Antiracist Research that Boston University has provided Ibram Kendi with is, in focusing on Kendi's *religious* approach to racism, a divinity school. It has been provided for someone whose formal credentials are those of a scholar but whose actual function in society is that of a priest.

The Elect have original sin.

The Elect, then, have magic, clergy, and also a conception of original sin. Under Elect creed, the sin is "white privilege."

To anticipate a question, yes, I do believe that to be white in America is to automatically harbor certain unstated privileges in terms of one's sense of belonging. Figures of authority are the same color as you. You are thought of as the default category. You are not subject to stereotypes. Although these days, you actually are subject to one—that of the menacing, anal "whiteness" monster the Elect tar you as—but we shall not quibble.

But the issue here is not whether I or anyone else thinks white privilege is real, but what we consider *the proper response to it*. The Elect are to ritually "acknowledge" that they possess white privilege, with an awareness that they can never be absolved of it. Classes, seminars, and teach-ins are devoted to corralling whites into this approach to the matter. The Elect seek to inculcate white kids with their responsibility to acknowledge their privilege from as early an age as possible; as I write this, religion is being preached in one school after another nationwide, even to children who aren't even reading chapter books yet. In other words, the Elect are founding the equivalent of Sunday school—except that, because they have penetrated actual schools, they get to preach at our children five days a week.

And oh, imagine the texts this publicly funded Sunday school approach will offer. Robin DiAngelo's *White Fragility* seeks to convert whites to a profound reconception of themselves as inherently complicit in a profoundly racist system of operation and thought. Within this system, if whites venture any statement on the topic other than that they harbor white privilege, it only proves that they are racists, too "fragile" to admit it. The circularity here—"You're a racist, and if you say you aren't, it just proves that you are"—is the logic of the sandbox.

Yet the book became a runaway bestseller in 2020, ballyhooed as a seminal text by the Elect and bringing countless converts into their flock. The only coherent explanation for so many people treating such a blatantly self-contradictory text as worthy of such attention is superstition. Many who are reading this book picked up *White Fragility* and were baffled at its reception. You need not be: *White Fragility* is a primer on original sin, no more baffling than the New Testament.

Nominally, one acknowledges original sin as a preparation for admittance to living in the grace of Jesus after death. On the ground, however, a person often lives within a narrower concern—whether or not one is a good person here on this earth—for reasons connected to our everyday experiences and how we appear to others as we go through them. In the same way, this acknowledgment of white privilege is framed as a prelude to activism, but in practice, the acknowledgment itself is the main meal. Despite formal claims otherwise, in real life the Elect testify—yes, testify—to their white privilege as a self-standing, totemic act.

People supposedly committed to political transformation breezily ignore the yawningly abstract relationship between testifying to "privilege" and forging change in the real world. At one meeting at Northwestern University's law school in 2020, professors actually stood up and ritually denounced themselves as not only harboring privilege but as being outright racists. All were required to do this regardless of individual nature or political commitments, leading an observer to say of one professor, "He is a wonderful man universally loved by students. It makes me sad that he is forced to say otherwise."

It won't do to sideline the law faculty of a top-ranked university as mere "kooks" whose behavior signals nothing about the tenor of the era, and the burden is on the skeptic to explain how this is anything *but* the original sin concept in translation, complete with the ineradicability. One is born marked by original sin; in the same way, to be white is to be born with the stain of unearned privilege. The proper response to original sin is to embrace the teachings of Jesus, although one will remain always a sinner nevertheless. The proper response to white privilege is to embrace the teachings of Ta-Nehisi Coates, Ibram Kendi, and Robin DiAngelo (and surely other prophet-priests by the time you read this and beyond), with the understanding that you will always harbor the privilege stain nevertheless.

We see this especially clearly in white people as they lustily pump their fists and do high fives with like-minded pals over the writings of a Coates who says that he is surprised that white people—i.e., they—are interested enough in black people and racism to even bother reading his work, and who saw the white firefighters who died on 9/11 as getting their just deserts. These same readers' friends, in 2020, were often seen posting photos of themselves on social media, holding a copy of *White Fragility*, showing their comrades that they were "doing the work." Coates and DiAngelo are calling these people sinners. Yet the sinners eagerly drink in the charge, revering their accusers, and come away from this self-mortification feeling energized. *Cleansed.*

This is worship, by people embracing the self-mortification of the inveterate sinner, stained by the original sin of white privilege.

The Elect are evangelical.

"Why don't they allow people to have different opinions?"

You're missing the point. The Elect can seem truly baffling—until we see that they are a religion. Specifically, an evangelical one.

To wit: Do we wonder why fundamentalist Christians do not see their beliefs as just one of many valid opinions? They see themselves as bearers of a Good News that, if all people would simply open up and see it, would create a perfect world. That most of the world does not fall in with them is something they learn to bear with toleration, with a hope that in the future things will turn their way. We see a certain coherence in Christians who view the rest of us as "heathen." We may disagree, but we can easily imagine someone under the impression that their worldview—if it includes unreachable belief in things we never see or feel that they insist are real nevertheless—is truth, while ours is an error. Christianity (or one of the other Abrahamic religions) is something many of us grow up around, or at least know of, from an early age. It feels normal. Because it is.

To be Elect is to think in exactly the same way. Key to being Elect is a sense that there is always a flock of unconverted heathen. Many of the heathen are, for example, the whites "out there," as it is often put about the white people who were so widely feared as possibly keeping Barack Obama from being elected (twice). The Elect wonder how those people "out there" can be reached. They are, from a Mormon perspective, behind doors as yet un–knocked upon.

Note that people might refer to whites "out there" when speaking from any place in this country. It is not only coastals with the Midwest in mind who call this other set of whites "out there." People use this expression in Chicago, Louisville, Portland, Madison, and Atlanta. Nor is it only an urban/rural issue—for example, a New Yorker referring to sketchy whites "out there" might be talking about whites living in the heart of Birmingham, Alabama, or El Paso, Texas, or even Staten Island. The people in question are *out* as compared with what is thought of as *in here*—in here where we are blessed with the true wisdom, a womb of sorts, where we live bathed in the grace of . . . well, let's just have it as *in here where we "get it,"* ritually atoning for our stain of white privilege.

It is easy to see smugness in this vision, and to wonder how so very many people could fall so easily into being so insufferable. We need not see them this way. They are not smug. They are evangelists. They are normal—as are all religious people.

The Elect are apocalyptic.

Elect scripture stipulates a judgment day: the great day when America "owns up to" or "comes to terms with" racism and finally fixes it. Apparently this will happen through the long-term effects of psychological self-mortification combined with the transformational political activism that whites will be moved to effect upon being morally shamed and verbally muzzled.

Notice that this makes no real sense? And besides, how would a country as massive, heterogenous, and politically fractured as this one ever arrive at a consensus so conclusive and overarching that it would "fix" racism? The whites "out there" are such incorrigible heathens, we are told. Okay, but if so, just what were we assuming would change their minds? Reading *White Fragility*? Try again. Tablets from on high sounds almost more plausible.

And notice that the Elect find such questions unwelcome, or even arrogant, as if they are asking how we dare question the divine. Even the language here is liturgical, referring only approximately to actual existence, and fully comprehensible only as poetry, spirit, or prophecy. So, to venture some additional arrogance: What would it mean for America to "come to terms" with racism? Precisely what configuration, event, or consensus would this coming to terms consist of? Who would determine that the terms had actually been come to? Why should we assume that the Elect would ever allow that the terms *had* been come to? They are, after all, obsessively condemnatory of any attempts to come to any today—they teach us that any sense we have that progress is happening is just another form of racism and "fragility," and are professionally resistant to allowing that any real progress has happened.

On the ground, the Elect imperative is to insist how far we are from this great day, mired in a present within which nothing changes. Why? Because the fantasy of an America ever just a half inch past *Plessy v. Ferguson* creates an urgency that justifies extreme action. Catastrophizing the current moment is a hallmark of ideology; in 1951, Eric Hoffer's *The True Believer* noted that movements such as Fascism, Communism, and nineteenth-century segregationists have attracted and retained their followers by appealing to an idealized past, a fantastical future, and an indelibly polluted present. Under the Elect, black people's noble past is Africa; the glorious future is about those *terms* that we will *come to*; while the present, if the religion is to make any kind of sense, must always be a cesspool.

The general idea that America is in some kind of denial about race—or racism, which is what people really mean when they say this—is perfectly absurd. America is nothing less than obsessed with discussing and acknowledging racism, and those who insist year after year that America wants to hear nothing of it are dealing in pure fantasy. America has most certainly not heeded the Elect's particular and eccentric requirements on race and racism, but to phrase this as a general neglect of the whole topic is not a matter of mere sloppiness; it's a willful commitment to believing something demonstrably untrue.

As I write this in 2021, America has become conscious of racism, within just a year, to a degree so extreme, so sustained, and so sincere that history offers no parallel, either in this country or any other. Besides organizations nationwide airing statements in support of Black Lives Matter, whether or not their business has anything to do with race relations, Netflix's CEO has donated $120 million to historically black colleges and universities and Hulu is putting one episode of Padma Lakshmi's food show *Taste the Nation* online for free: the one about the cuisine of the black people of South Carolina's Sea Islands. Confederate statues are coming down not just one at a time but in droves. The Associated Press has decided to capitalize the word *Black*. Merriam-Webster is revising its definition of *racism* to include modern definitions focusing on disparities rather than attitudes. The term *master bedroom*, tech designations like *master drive* and *slave drive*, and even golf's Masters Tournament are being reconsidered. Suddenly the entire nation is aware of, and helping black America to celebrate, the holiday Juneteenth, with many cities giving black people the day off as a paid holiday. In many of the protests in the wake of George Floyd's murder, so many of the faces are white that you'd think the movement was sponsored by Greenpeace.

The 1619 Project in *The New York Times*, despite the conclusive determination that it is founded on a mistaken interpretation of the historical record, has been awarded a Pulitzer Prize, out of the tacit Elect assumption that when it comes to race, indignation outranks accuracy. Black Lives Matter protests in solidarity with the ones here are taking place in countries where many of the protesters don't speak much English and have never known a black American. Congress—the deadlocked travesty that is our Congress in the twenty-first century—has passed a bill encouraging serious police reform. Minneapolis, where Floyd was killed, vowed to dismantle its entire police force, while nationwide a debate rages over whether the police should be defunded to a radical degree.

Nationwide, prominent whites are examining themselves for abusive "whiteness," such that Tina Fey has pulled four episodes of her beloved sitcom *30 Rock* from streaming because it had quick blackface gags. Comic actress Jenny Slate has withdrawn from providing the voice of a biracial character on the series *Big Mouth*. Disneyland has retooled its Splash Mountain ride to highlight *The Princess and the Frog*, with its black princess Tiana, instead of the controversial *Song of the South*. New York City has painted BLACK LIVES MATTER in big letters right down the street in front of Trump Tower.

White attitudes on race and the prevalence of racism were dramatically different in 2020 than they had been just a few years before. A Monmouth University poll showed that while 50 percent of whites in 2015 thought racism was a serious problem for black people, by last year 71 percent did. This shift in attitude helped deny reelection to the openly bigoted president Donald Trump. The racial reckoning of 2020 also drove Joe Biden's choice of a black woman as his running mate, and Kamala Harris may well become the next president herself.

And yet notice that, to the Elect, none of this has mattered a whit.

The same kinds of people are saying the same kinds of things about how black people are unheard, unseen, that America never "comes to terms" with race. One hears that Kamala Harris is only the *vice* president, after all, and was chosen by an old white man. Or that while Trump is out, we'd better not think his influence doesn't remain in force. The despair is unchanged. Asked if there has been a sea change since 2020, they hesitantly admit that what happened was "welcome" or "a beginning"—but only that.

To these people, actual progress on race is not something to celebrate but to talk around. This is because, with progress, the Elect lose their sense of purpose. Note: What they are after is not money or power, but sheer purpose, in the basic sense of feeling like you matter and that your life has a meaningful agenda. Take the idea that even if Trump didn't win a second term, he did win a first one, it wasn't that long ago, he did not lose by a landslide, and the racism in America suggested by all of this is "what we really need to be talking about." No, this is not a hypothetical: Hot on the heels of President Biden's inauguration, Ta-Nehisi Coates published an article titled "Donald Trump Is Out. Are We Ready to Talk About How He Got In?"

Cue the applause—but wait. Never mind the notion that no one had been ready to "talk about" something that was actually mulled over utterly, thoroughly, and unceasingly for the entire four years Trump was in office. More to the point: Why, exactly, do race issues mean that startling developments in the present are less worthy of real discussion than gloomy history lessons? The reason we supposedly "really need to be talking about" 2016 over 2020 is because 2020 was good news, but 2016 was Good News in the Christian meaning of the term—as in, a message about racism lingering and in need of battling. Good News is gooder than good—i.e., real—news.

If by chance the new mood leads to an actual reparations program, a worthy guess is that the new memes will be things like "Reparations is just a start" and "They better not think they can treat us like animals for four hundred years and just pay us off." You don't have to take my word for it. Coates is useful again, giving it away long ago in his famed article on reparations, where he ventured that "we may find that the country can never fully repay African Americans." Or: There has been a proposal that an algorithm could provide a principled and systematic way of computing the amount of reparations payments black people should receive. A black writer has objected that this could never work, and not because of something about the mechanics of the algorithm, but because it couldn't address the sheer spiritual *pain* that slavery and its aftermath caused. But then, what could?

Randall Robinson's book led to the same kind of conclusion. He argued that slavery "has hulled empty a whole race of people with inter-generational efficiency. Every artifact of the victims' past cultures, every custom, every ritual, every god, every language, every trace element of a people's whole hereditary identity, wrenched from them and ground into a sharp choking dust." Well, okay . . . but then, his idea of what reparations would consist of is (1) an education trust fund, (2) recovery of funds from companies that benefited from slave labor, (3) general support for "civil rights advocacy," and (4) financial amends to the Caribbean and Africa. These would be good things, but they would do very little to heal the utter sociopsychological annihilation Robinson thought all black people labor under. It follows that he thought reparations could accomplish very little actual repair.

The Elect talk endlessly about the power of language and imagery related to race issues. But after the language and imagery on race are massively transformed nationwide, they sit unappeased, jaws set, now dismissing changes in language and imagery as mere fiddling with surfaces, incanting the same mantras they were before. For them, black lives matter, but seismic sociopolitical transformation in how black people are perceived does not.

Thus, a professional historian and former president of Harvard can casually end a thoughtful piece on William Faulkner by referring to "the shameful history we have still failed to confront or understand." No editor at the magazine Drew Gilpin Faust was writing for deigned to challenge such a hopelessly fantastical depiction of America, despite that this piece was written months after the protests over George Floyd's murder. A failure to confront or understand? This refers to nothing real, but because it was not intended to, we let sentences like that pass.

Then, in February of 2021, here was an insight from a black historian (and university president) about how far we had come by then:

> The erasure is as stunning as it is thorough. The role of Black labor in building the Southern economic infrastructure has been routinely denied. The contributions that Black scholars have made in the humanities, the life sciences, and the natural sciences have been lost because of segregated workplaces. The work of Black creative

artists has been disregarded since it became appropriated into the national cultural apparatus.

Denied, lost, disregarded—all couched in the artful use of the perfect tense: These things *have been* denied, not *were* denied. The perfect tense implies that the past reaches into the present—*Elvis has left the building* versus *Elvis left the building*—allowing this writer to imply that what happened eons ago is still on some level something that *is* rather than *was*.

Yet this almost fantastical pessimism was predictably celebrated by the usual suspects as thrilling testimony. This kind of thing makes sense only as a willful refusal to allow that real change happens. Sociopolitical progress is irrelevant to the Elect's take on race in America not because they are stubborn, not because they profit somehow from stirring people up, but because antiracism is their religious faith.

My assumption that the Elect will be unmoved by what happened during 2020 and beyond will seem hubristic. But in the end, the simple question is whether I'm right—upon which I merely ask you to look around.

See?

The Elect ban the heretic.

The Elect consider it imperative to not only critique those who disagree with their creed, but to seek their punishment and elimination to whatever degree real-life conditions can accommodate.

There is an overriding sense that unbelievers must be not just spoken out against, but called out, isolated, and banned.

To many this looks hasty, immature, unconsidered. It is much of why the Elect are often minimized in public perception as mostly people under twenty-five or so. Surely it is hotheaded kids full of beans who behave this way, rather than seasoned adults?

Alas, no. The reality is that what the Elect call *problematic* is what a Christian means by *blasphemous*. The Elect do not ban people out of temper; they do it calmly, between sips of coffee as they surf Twitter, because they consider it a higher wisdom to burn witches.

Not literally, but the sentiment is the same. The Elect are members of a religion, of a kind within which the dissenter is not just someone in disagreement but is a kind of environmental pollution. They are not to be among us. As Andrew Sullivan noted about his having to leave his post at *New York* magazine in 2020, it had gotten to the point that the Elect staffers found his very presence unbearable:

> They seem to believe, and this is increasingly the orthodoxy in mainstream media, that any writer not actively committed to critical theory in questions of race, gender, sexual orientation, and gender identity is actively, physically harming co-workers merely by existing in the same virtual space.

A sad amount of ink has been spilled over the idea that such people must stop being so delicate, that they are fragile creatures deformed by helicopter parenting. The truth is that this is not real fragility, but a pose. The Elect do not feel frightened, much less physically injured, by columns, tweets, syllabi, symbols, and verbal expressions. They are posing as injured in order to demonstrate the "violence" of the views with which they disagree and thus prove that those views are evil. This use of the concept of violence takes a page from, first, the writings of Michel Foucault and, second, intelligent discussions among radical feminists in the 1980s and '90s. But it retools them as a way of enforcing what earlier human societies knew as taboo.

People who find working at the same organization as a thinker like Sullivan intolerable—and this was not in a physical office pool but in a largely virtual space during the quarantine!—are recapitulating those who expel the heretic by making a cross with their fingers. The religious fervor is absolutist, complete with a Manichaean sense of good versus evil. Many recall Dana Carvey's Church Lady on *Saturday Night Live*, with her self-celebratory obsession with smoking out the doings of "SATAN?!" The people who chased Andrew Sullivan away from *New York* magazine and Bari Weiss from *The New York Times* (they resigned in persecution from their institutions during the same week in mid-2020) would laugh at the kind of person Carvey was channeling, unaware that they engage in the exact same behavior.

As Glenn Loury has suggested during one of our discussions online, whenever you hear the Elect deem someone "problematic," to understand what they are saying and hold them accountable for it, substitute the word *witch*. "Well, isn't what X is saying problematic in that . . . [sip latte]" is another way of saying, with nothing whatsoever lost or added in the translation, "Well, doesn't what X is saying make her a witch?"

Caricature! Overstatement! Okay, but behold this faculty letter, from a body of PhDs—*PhDs*—at Princeton, one passage from a suite of demands submitted to the university president (who was in warm agreement with ideas of this kind):

> Constitute a committee composed entirely of faculty that would oversee the investigation and discipline of racist behaviors, incidents, research, and publication on the part of faculty, following a protocol for grievance and appeal to be spelled out in Rules and Procedures of the Faculty. Guidelines on what counts as racist behavior, incidents, research, and publication will be authored by a faculty committee for incorporation into the same set of rules and procedures.

If this isn't a star chamber, I don't know what is. This was a proposal for a committee of anti-heresy, pure and simple. As time goes on, many readers will wonder whether the paragraph is a hoax. But it was real, penned and signed by living persons otherwise going home to feed children, mow the lawn, and catch up on season two of *Succession*.

In 2019, the media coalesced around calling the Elect's behavior "cancel culture." The Elect's pushback by 2020 was perfectly revealing. They often stated that they had no desire to "cancel" people but insisted on their right to speak out against those they disagreed with. However, people of this mindset typically assume, without the slightest question, that "speaking against" must include attempts to punish, to strip people of titles, to strip people of their epaulettes.

One sensed that they were not aware that just some years before, there was no such assumption, among anything like so large a group, that people deserved punishment beyond *being taken to task* for views deemed unsavory. This was not evidence of people being strangely selfish or pushy; it was evidence that they were being guided by a religion that coalesced during the 2010s and crystallized in the wake of George Floyd's murder, under which a dissenting view must be not just questioned but quashed, there being no possible good world that includes it. It takes very little time before people in their maturity don't remember what things were like rather recently.

Why can't they allow other views? Remember, this is religion, not political science, and specifically a religion eerily akin to devout Christianity. To the Elect, racism is the equivalent of Satan. If I deign to walk by Satan with the idea that we can just let him be, I am missing the point. I am "wrong."

A quick look at a real Elect person up close will illustrate further. Someone once tweeted about me in passing that I am opposed to black people's quest for equality. I want to be clear that my purpose here is not to air grievance: People have said much worse about me over decades, they are doing so as you read this, and they will continue to do so. However, it's safe to say that most people who are familiar with what I do would be hard-pressed to see me as someone standing grimly and saying, "Black people should not seek to be equal with whites."

What would lead me to dislike the idea of other black people being treated as equals? One might fashion a notion of me as a sinister figure who thinks that, aside from myself, black people are somehow inherently inferior. But how many of us have seen anyone actually like this outside of a *Boondocks* cartoon? Who, if asked to actually defend that portrait of me with examples, could do so—in a way that most readers would *sincerely* consider valid?

Here is the heuristic value of that tweet: She is a college professor. She mentors students, writes academic articles, serves on committees, and surely sees herself as valuing a diversity of ideas. She likely loves her parents, has hobbies. There is a kind of person who can function as a bright, civil, and loving person while also sending gratuitously prosecutorial tweets like that. It's as if some kind of virus implanted in them makes them commit acts otherwise alien to their nature, like the little worm larvae that burrow into a grasshopper's brain. The worms are aquatic when they mature, and they transform the grasshopper's brain such that it jumps into water and dies, allowing the worms to emerge into the water, where they thrive.

There must be an override, in other words, that makes nice people write things like this. Elect ideology stipulates that one's central moral duty is to battle racism and the racist. My opinions on race do not always fit that bill: while I earnestly seek strategies to improve black lives, I do not focus on doing so by identifying and battling white bias or deeming society at large as a racist "system" that must be somehow disassembled—these approaches strike me as too unlikely to bear fruit. But the Elect take on race is founded on a religious requirement to decry racism rather than on seeking and measuring the results of efforts to make black people's lives better. As such, under their perspective, my views qualify as errors. In not adhering to their tenets, I am committing the sin of countering their gospel, dismissing the mission that they see as rendering them and other people worthy as human beings. As such, I am a foe, someone who is "against" them—and thus, by extension, "against" black equality.

It cannot be logic that leads a sane person to send out a senseless character-assassinating graffito and then go about her perfectly normal day. If we are to grant her the dignity of assessing her as an intelligent, moral person—and we must, and we do—her tweet was a form of *testifying* as a member of the Elect.

We look at the signers of the petitions seeking to drag someone into the stocks and think, "*He* signed this?" We wonder why that mild-mannered woman we met at the faculty mixer was on the committee that came close to deep-sixing the career of a liberal professor who did nothing wrong. We watch a Twitter or Facebook mob tearing at someone's entrails and notice a perfectly wonderful, pacific, and brilliant acquaintance of ours happily "liking" the invective and even pitching in. That is because Electism is a religion, not a riot. It knows all types.

Thus, when America entered upon what was often termed a

period of racial reckoning after the Floyd tragedy, the Elect commonly justified their witch burnings as unquestionably in line with the reckoning in question. It was rather stunning to see their blithe assumption that any racial reckoning of worth must include chasing people out of conversations and casting people into unemployment, without seeing it as necessary to even defend any of this. But that's just it: For the Elect, barring heretics is not a decision. It is duty—unquestioned, and as natural as breathing air.

A person is usually not given to thinking outside of their religion, of imagining what thought was like before the religion existed. A religion is all-consuming, and in this case makes the difference between 1992 political correctness's "I find that offensive" and the Elect of 2020's "Tar and feather them." Drifting from a commitment to changing society toward a narrower commitment to signaling antipathy to racism and leaving it there, antiracism's progress from its First to its Third waves has taken it from the concrete political activism of Martin Luther King to the faith-based commitments of a Martin Luther.

The Elect supplant older religions.

Daniel Patrick Moloney, the Massachusetts Institute of Technology's Catholic chaplain, in line with his profession and his religion, wrote an email gently suggesting that even cops who murder be viewed with some attempt at understanding their humanity and why they stray from the good. After noting the horror of Floyd's murder and the culpability of the officer who killed him, Moloney ventured:

> Many people have claimed that racism is a major problem in police forces. I don't think we know that. Police officers deal with dangerous and bad people all the time, and that often hardens them. They do this so that the rest of us can live in peace, but sometimes at a cost to their souls.

The language of those who came after him was indicative. One tweet: "First order of business, lets talk about Fr. Maloney (MIT Catholic Chaplain) and the email he thought it was ok to send today." Note the "he thought it was ok to send," with its air of censure by a tribunal of prelates who decide what is permissible to say versus what isn't.

A follow-up tweet: "I am truly sorry to any black Catholics at MIT y'all deserve so much better (sad face emoji)," followed by the first tweeter intoning, "Exactly, which is why he should be removed. He clearly can't serve students of color safely and effectively . . . so he can't serve at all." But how could that gentle homily Moloney wrote make anyone "unsafe"? It's a huge jump, one that perplexes onlookers—does this person truly believe that an email calling for caution and understanding could be the cause of another black man getting killed by a cop? Such a fear would make so little sense it is inconceivable even for someone who is mentally unwell.

This tweeter was working from the Elect conception of ideas beyond their orbit being heretical. Only persecuting those deemed racist passes muster; anything else, by definition, encourages racism by not combatting it.

"So he can't serve at all," that tweeter closed with. And off Galileo goes to house arrest—we are watching the Inquisition in miniature. Moloney had to resign.

This Elect imperative has infected Unitarianism quite a bit as well, attracting comment from within that neatly illustrates the nature of the mindset. Reverend Richard Trudeau has watched the "zombie" phenomenon:

> These leaders—at the Unitarian Universalist Association, in our two seminaries, and in the UU Ministers' Association—have become so committed and intransigent that I have started to think of the ideology that has captivated them as a *mental virus* with which they have become infected. By this analogy I do not mean to imply that they are mentally ill, of course, but only that they seem stuck in a rut (think Communism, 1917-1989). Victims of this mental virus can be recognized by their calls to "dismantle our white supremacy culture."

Reverend Todd Eklof, similarly alarmed, wrote a book, part of which critiqued this new Elect element in Unitarianism. The Unitarian Universalist Ministers Association censured and expelled him for it; he was also expelled from the Unitarian Universalist Fellowship and barred from supervising ministerial interns, leaving Unitarian ministers nationwide with any skepticism of Elect ideology worried about speaking out.

The historian of religion will find 2020 illustrative as a time when American Christianity in many places began a slow transition into a new Elect version of itself. For example, the pastor of New York City's Church of St. Francis Xavier led vows addressing white privilege and racial justice, melding Catholicism and Electism on the level of personal testimony in a fashion much more reminiscent of *White Fragility* than Dorothy Day. Around the same time, a black teen at the Black Lives Matter protest site in Seattle had himself recorded telling whites that black people are "holier"—which is quite true within the Elect hierarchy in which whites are Satan on top, while sainthood increases with all other people as you move down the hierarchy of intersectional oppression.

And so it goes.

It's all water from the same well. What seem like disparate events, or scattered actions by people who have for some reason "gone crazy," are all products of the agenda of a body of people united around a new religion they seek to found a new America upon. Here are some other things that fall under the same analysis, serving as a kind of slice-of-life tour of what 2020 felt like regarding race issues.

1. New York City mayor Bill de Blasio genuflected to the Elect in sanctioning ongoing protests despite the quarantine order. Legions of protesters were taking

to the streets nationwide for weeks on end, often huddled close together, often maskless, yelling and chanting at length despite a virus easily spread via water droplets from the mouth. De Blasio had broken up a Hasidic wedding for breaking the recommended social distancing rules, but weeks later he was fine with people breaking the same rules in much larger numbers and for much longer when the issue was battling racism. In his own words: "When you see a nation, an entire nation, simultaneously grappling with an extraordinary crisis seeded in 400 years of American racism, I'm sorry, that is not the same question as the understandably aggrieved store owner or the devout religious person who wants to go back to services."

This was piety, of exactly the kind that motivated the religious people he mentioned. This secular person in authority let pass such protests even in view of an extremely dangerous virus that had already killed thousands of people in his city alone. This was because Elect ideology, with its power to override even scientific fact if things bring the conflict to a head, is a religion.

And de Blasio wasn't alone. In one of the most medieval moments in modern American history, medical professionals refrained from condemning this behavior, often even openly venturing that battling racism was more important than *avoiding the trans-*

mission of a grievously destructive virus. Few of these medical professionals were likely Elect themselves, but they cowered enough under its power to act like they were. It was a uniquely eloquent refutation of the Elect's tendency to dismiss critique as overestimating their impact.

2. A friend wrote on Facebook that they agree with Black Lives Matter, only to be roasted by an anonymous person:

> *Wait a minute! You "agree" with them? That implies you get to disagree with them! That's like saying you "agree" with the law of gravity! You as a white person don't get to "agree" OR "disagree" when black people assert something! Saying you "agree" with them is EVERY bit as arrogant as disputing them! This isn't an intellectual exercise! This is THEIR lives on the line!*

This objection seems studiously hostile. But then, beyond a certain point, one is not to think one's way through a *dogma* in logical fashion, from A to Z, and decide whether it makes sense. At a certain point you are to suspend logic and have faith. The problem is that this Facebook commenter and so many others actually think it is progress for their religion to become America's new foundation.

A parallel event in 2020: A Taco Bell employee wearing a face mask with BLM written on it was asked by management to change it, based on a rule that employees were not to bring politics into the workplace. Elect Twitter (as opposed to Twitter; we must distinguish) was alight with people objecting that Black Lives Matter is not politics—in other words, that Black Lives Matter's positions are unquestionable truth, rendering irrelevant all matters of etiquette or regulation. This bar on matters of logic, even with a smile, is what is known as religion.

3. In the wake of the murder of George Floyd, it became newly common to see white people actually adopting religious body language in fealty to black people, with black people often present and standing in attendance. In Bethesda, Maryland, white protesters against Floyd's murder knelt on the pavement en masse, chanting allegiance to anti-white-privilege tenets incanted by what could only be deemed the pastor of the flock, all with hands actually up in the air. Social media recorded another episode in which white protesters actually bowed down to black people standing right in front of them as they received their antiracism testaments, many in tears. White protesters washed their fellow black protesters' feet in Cary, North Carolina (yes, this actually happened!), while elsewhere, many black protesters sensed some performativity in white activists strolling around with

painted whip scars on their bodies, to show their sympathy for the black condition.

4. Meanwhile, nominally secular institutions have openly advocated religious orientation toward race issues as if they were the divinity schools that all universities once essentially were. A professor at the Steinhardt School at New York University distributed a memo actually stating outright that "our first guiding principle is that participation in political movements such as Black Lives Matter is analogous to a decision to attend a religious or spiritual gathering"—and no, he is not a theologian or even a social scientist, but a statistics professor! Allegheny College's statement of allegiance to the racial reckoning included the plea "We humbly ask for grace and patience. We are imperfect and will make mistakes," in language quite reminiscent of a prayer or psalm.

THIS IS A RELIGIOUS FAITH. It has a creation myth: that all of today's problems with race trace to the first Africans being brought to our shores in 1619, and the Revolutionary War was fought because Britain was moving toward abolishing slavery, despite leading historians noting the inaccuracy of the historical premise. There is what we could think of as a triple-testament tome, consisting of Ta-Nehisi Coates's *Between the World and*

Me, Robin DiAngelo's *White Fragility*, and Ibram Kendi's *How to Be an Antiracist*. A box set of the three would take its place on coffee tables and mantelpieces nationwide. And Electism is a *successful* creed, quite compellingly evangelical. Its adherents make Americans more religious by the year—and this possibly includes you.

One does not have to explicitly call oneself religious to merit the description. Until the sixteenth and seventeenth centuries, Europeans who believed fervently in God, Jesus and his resurrection, angels, Satan, and miracles did not think of themselves as "religious" but as ordinary. Only with scientific progress, encounters with other peoples of the world with radically different beliefs, and the demystifying aspects of the Reformation did there emerge a sense that adherence to a certain set of Christian tenets was "religious" as opposed to empirical. Electism forces us to think like people of the Dark Ages without knowing it. It's scary, it's unfair and regressive, and it's just plain wrong.

America's sense of what it is to be intellectual, moral, or artistic, what it is to educate a child, what it is to foster justice, what it is to express oneself properly, and what it is to be a nation is being refounded upon a religion. This is directly antithetical to the very foundations of the American experiment. Religion has no place in the classroom, in the halls of ivy, in our codes of ethics, or in decreeing how all members of society are to express themselves, and almost all of us spontaneously understand that and see any misunderstanding of the premise as backward. Yet, since about 2015, a peculiar contingent is slowly headlocking us into making an exception, supposing that this particular new religion is so incontestably correct, so gorgeously surpassing millennia of brilliant philosophers' attempts to identify the ultimate morality, that we can only bow down in humble acquiescence.

The point of this book is to delineate a certain modern way of thinking as less progressive than peculiar, as something we must learn to step around and resist rather than let pass as a kind of higher wisdom. A cohesive and forward-looking society must treat this kind of thought like a virus, a regrettable though perhaps inevitable result of modern social history, which nevertheless must be ongoingly corralled. We should hope for its eventual disappearance, but if this is impossible—and it likely is—it must be kept on the margins of our existence, just as smallpox is.

A new religion in the guise of world progress is not an advance; it is a detour. It is not altruism; it is self-help. It is not sunlight; it is fungus. It's time it became ordinary to call it for what it is and stop cowering before it, letting it make people so much less than they—black and everything else—could be. There is nothing correct about the essence of American thought and culture being transplanted into the soil of a religious faith. Some will go as far as to own up to it being a religion and wonder why we can't just accept it as our new national creed. The problem is that on matters of societal procedure and priorities, the adherents of this religion—true to the very nature of religion—cannot be reasoned with. They are, in this, medievals with lattes.

Question these people for real and they howl as if having a finger pulled backward. But it isn't that they don't want their power taken away: The Elect see themselves as speaking truth *to* power, not as occupying it. What they perceive as threatened is their reason for being, as engaged humans in this world. We cannot hate them for that, but our problem is the vast gulf between their sense of personal mission and the rest of ours, and the fact that their mission includes the tool of calling people racists in the public square.

We are genuinely in *Invasion of the Body Snatchers* territory. The Elect will insist that the term *religion* diminishes them, but the simple propositions of this chapter make it painfully clear that whether they like hearing it or not, Electism is very much a new religion, but one conducted in a language that misdirects us by misfiling the phenomenon under labels like *politics* and *commitments* and *social justice*. Adoring their kids, poaching their salmon, strumming their ukuleles barefooted, savoring their Stones and Coldplay and Adele, they may seem unlike what we think of as "religious." But don't be fooled: Religion knows no culture. Nor do all religions entail the worship of a God (the Elect lack one), or even forgiveness (which the Elect do not seem to have exactly caught up with just yet). As Eric Hoffer put it, religions don't need a God, but they need a devil, and the Elect have that down quite comfortably. Superstition, clergy, sinfulness, a proselytizing impulse, a revulsion against the impure—it's all there. They think of it all as logic incarnate.

But so, as he lustily led the Spanish Inquisition, did Torquemada.

3

WHAT ATTRACTS PEOPLE TO THIS RELIGION?

F ROM A CERTAIN DISTANCE it looks like we are dealing with people who "went crazy." But that won't do. How many people can we realistically tar as insane? In what human society has a critical mass of people ever become mentally deranged? Yet we want to know just why this new religion arose.

A religion soothes. It helps people make sense of things. The question is why this particular religion, promulgated so often with such sneering contempt, soothes so many. First we need to take a look at the rootstock of this movement.

Critical race theory says what?

Critical race theory started with developments among a certain group of legal scholars a few decades ago. At that time, no one was chanting George Floyd's name while torpedoing someone for tenure in an academic department, or while suspending someone from a newspaper, or while excommunicating someone for holding "problematic"—i.e., blasphemous—views.

The difference between good old-fashioned left and modern Elect began to emerge when, for example, legal scholar Richard Delgado began teaching non-whites to base their complaints about injustice not on something so "rigid" as objective truth, but upon the "broad story of dashed hopes and centuries-long mistreatment that afflicts an entire people and forms the historical and cultural background of your complaint."

This kind of argument was the source for the one now so familiar, that if a brown person says they have encountered racism, then it is automatically indisputable that they did, and if you don't agree it makes you "problematic."

Another legal scholar, Regina Austin, outlined another plank in this philosophy:

A new politics of identification, fueled by critically confronting the question of the positive significance of black lawbreaking, might restore some vitality to what has become a mere figure of speech. . . . Drawing on lawbreaker culture would add a bit of toughness, resilience, bluntness, and defiance to contemporary mainstream black political discourse, which evidences a marked preoccupation with civility, respectability, sentimentality, and decorum.

In other words, politics needs a jolt of some gott-damned *street*! Yes, this was from a scholar of jurisprudence, and its like was the fount of the idea that for brown people, the old rules don't matter. Forget (fuck?) civility or even logic (see Delgado, above)—it's all about how you feel, and specifically about how you hate the reigning order. Critical race theory tells you that everything is about hierarchy, power, their abuses—and that if you are not Caucasian in America, then you are akin to the captive oarsman slave straining belowdecks in chains.

Almost anyone can see what a reductive view this is of modern society, even without having read their Rousseau or Rawls. We must not be taken in by the fact that this is called "critical," that it's about race, and that it's titled a "theory." It is a fragile, performative ideology, one that goes beyond the passages above to explicitly reject linear reasoning, traditional legal theorizing, and even Enlightenment rationalism. We are to favor an idea that an oppressed race's "story" constitutes truth, in an overarching sense, apart from mere matters of empirical or individual detail.

If it seems odd that adults would ever have taken this seriously, it felt less fantastical as an outgrowth of deconstructionism in literary studies. This new way of reading—and, by extension, thinking—claimed that a text cannot convey any single truth, and that, rather, a text inevitably contains contradictions to its own claims, such that the nature of a text is the infinite messages that we draw from it as disparate readers. No text can firmly state anything.

All of this begins as an interesting challenge to what we think of as truth and even reality, requiring close reasoning, intelligent imagination, and even a sense of sociohistorical progressivism. The problem is that in real life, it has been diluted into things like the senseless self-contradictory Catechism of Contradictions we saw in chapter 1, presented as enlightenment. "CRT" is the root of the idea today, seemingly so senselessly manipulative, that any claim of racism a black person makes must qualify automatically as valid because . . . they are black and speaking from "their experience."

For anyone who perceives that this makes no sense at all because any human's take on something might be erroneous, they are unlikely to get a genuine explanation from people espousing it. The black person has usually internalized the assumption subconsciously and embraced it as almost any human would, as a tool that keeps people from disagreeing with you—who wouldn't find something like that at least preliminarily attractive? The white person embraces it as a way of showing how thoroughly they understand that racism exists (and, I suspect, often out of a quiet sense that if black people insist on this, they must, deep down, be somewhat cognitively deficient, and therefore the most humane strategy is to just placate).

Predictably, the typical law professor leaves CRT alone and hopes no one espousing it comes for them, as most people have better things to do than get called dirty names over something they care only so much about anyway. That its signature proponents have usually been people of color makes critiquing the "theory" especially forbidding to most. Those who deign to take on CRT beyond polite quibbles, if they do it where people will really hear it, are dismissed as racists or, if of color, just plain broken, as was black Harvard law professor Randall Kennedy in the wake of a 1989 article.

As such, its tenets have been free to trickle down into real life, to a point that most Elect have never even heard of the theoretical work itself, any more than those who espouse "rights" of various kinds typically can recite their Locke. CRT ideals now come baked into the hard left. Robin DiAngelo's *White Fragility*, for example, reads in the present tense like a bizarre exercise in mind control created by someone bent on manipulation and getting paid. That's a misinterpretation: It is a workbook based on principles foundational in seminars of critical race theory, which its author sincerely believes in, promoting it out of a sense of benevolent mission.

Or: Amid nationwide anti-cop protests, National Public Radio interviewed the author of a book called *In Defense of Looting* (no, not an *Onion* parody!). The book "attacks some of the core beliefs and structures of cisheteropatriarchal racial capitalist society" and argues that ownership rights are "not natural facts, but social constructs benefiting a few at the expense of the many, upheld by ideology, economy and state violence." So *burn, baby, burn* is progress? This way of looking at things traces directly to the kinds of prescriptions we saw Regina Austin putting forth.

There is no better illustration of this legacy than the proceedings of a New York City school board meeting in 2020, viewable online, in which perfectly sane people spout, in all earnestness, rhetoric straight out of the Elect playbook, singing of *White Fragility* and *How to Be an Antiracist* as if they were recovered epistles from Saint Peter, telling people to read them but unable to explain their tenets themselves, incapable of engaging in meaningful activity out of their unreachable intolerance of anyone who doesn't think the way they do.

The highlight of this session is a white Elect who waxes indignant at a white man who has a black child on his knee at the meeting, claiming that such sights hurt "them" (i.e., us poor black people, for whom seeing that is like watching our children being dandled by David Duke). Never mind that it turned out that this man was good friends with the child's mother and that their children were growing up together. Online, these Elect look, frankly, like self-satisfied idiots. However, they are ultimately innocent descendants of graduate students circa 1997 carrying their copies of Crenshaw, Gotanda, Peller, and Thomas (one of the signature early CRT anthologies).

Why do whites become Elects?

Thus, an obscure legal theory now feeds directly into a modus operandi that leads to indefensible suspensions, firings, and shamings nationwide, with its supporters seeing this, in all sincerity, as justice done in preparation for a brave new world.

But why would this way of thinking spread from law seminars into the rest of the world? What have people found so attractive about this way of thinking, that they not only adopt it as their life's creed but are even comfortable insulting, abusing, and destroying people on the basis of it?

This is an especially urgent question, in that critical race theory reads as especially "crazy" from the outside. I can think of few intellectual constructs that seem, on their face, less likely to seep into America's kitchens and living rooms (other than deconstruction, which didn't!). Critical race theory makes Marxism look like the ABCs. But here we are, with ordinary people channeling critical race theory tenets—and maybe even playing the ukulele! Why?

The answer differs according to whether one is white or, to use the term of the moment, BIPOC.

With whites, to be Elect is a natural outcome of the transformation of the left from what philosopher Richard Rorty termed in his *Achieving Our Country* a *reformist* left to a *cultural* left after the 1960s. This begins with a proposition that the American system is too rotten to merit reform, and that true justice will require our entire set of cultural values to change. As with literary deconstruction, this in itself is an interesting idea that deserves a "seat at the table." However, an almost inevitable outgrowth of it is an inward turn in its adherents, wherein one's commitment is driven more by *how it feels to be someone with the message* rather than the message alone.

As Rorty put it in that book, one comes to feel that self-expression is, in itself, a kind of persuasion, in that since you have the "proper" ideals, how you feel must, by itself, carry a certain moral and even logical authority. No human being can sit and review basic principles and their validity on a daily basis, and thus, after a while, this cultural leftist has come to suppose that his or her sentiments are a kind of political manifesto in themselves.

The result is what Nick Srnicek and Alex Williams have

called "folk politics," under which a prime attraction, embodied partly in the idea that to vent is to reason, is that we can "reduce complexity down to a human scale." Electism is presented as complex—i.e., in requiring the "work" we are told is necessary— but it is also, in being motivated by a simple quest to show that one is not a racist, rather easy. Easy is always attractive to all of us: Electism is a kind of politics hack.

Poet Czesław Miłosz captured that conformity lends an outright sense of pleasure and relief. Who among us doesn't enjoy a sense of having it all figured out? That rush of joy from solving an algebra problem, that sense of peace from figuring out the overriding reason that a romantic relationship went bust, or even the soothing feeling you get when first noticing that the app you downloaded onto your phone will also pop up on your iPad and you don't have to do it twice—to have a sense that all you have to do is push a button and everything falls into place can be a gorgeous thing.

Electism is one more in an endless succession of political philosophies offering this sense of coherence. It can exert even more of a siren call than many, such as Marxism, in its more immediate object of attention. The Marxist works for an abstract proletariat often difficult to motivate or even quite identify in real life. The Elect works for, as it were, George Floyd—he was no abstraction.

Of course, to be a proper Elect is to embrace a self-flagellational guilt for things you did not do. Yet even this, oddly, feels good. It is a brand of the "Western masochism" that philosopher Pascal Bruckner has taught us about. Pundit Douglas Murray nails it: "People imbibe because they like it," he tartly puts it. "It lifts them up and exalts them. Rather than being people responsible for themselves and answerable to those they know, they become the self-appointed representatives of the living and dead, the bearers of a terrible history as well as the potential redeemers of mankind. From being a nobody one becomes a somebody." Murray was referring to the left's take on Islam, but the analysis applies just as well to today's Elect take on black people.

Hence what Émile Durkheim called a "collective effervescence," amid which we find the explanation for the awkwardness of Elect whites being woker than most black people. Polls have shown this, and it is reflected in episodes such as the call for the World Scrabble Championship in 2020 to disallow the N-word and other slurs. This was a delicate issue lending itself to many views, but it was indicative that black Scrabble players tended to be less interested in expunging these slurs than were white ones.

Repeatedly, the Elect verge on telling black people—the supposed object of their veneration and eternal moral commitment—that they don't know what's good for them. For example, black people in tough neighborhoods commonly revile the idea that we ought to "defund" the police because of what happened to George Floyd and so many others. However, the Elect narrative—promoted heavily by mainstream media sources—sidelines this resistance as something that merely merits "consideration" (and of a kind that qualifies largely as dismissal). The condescension here is brutal, and what drives this squaring of the circle is religious fervor, complete with the sense of personal pleasure that it lends. The joy of finding order and of feeling important overrides how black people actually feel.

It is this kind of thing that leads so many to think the Elect are "crazy," but it has often been argued that Electism simply fills a hole left after the secular shift among thinking Americans especially after the 1960s. Under this analysis, it is human to need religious thought for a basic sense of succor, such that if institutional religion no longer grounds one's thought, then some similarly themed ideology will come in to serve in its place.

I will leave it to philosophers and theologians to explore that possibility in depth. However, it is hard not to see prescience in predictions such as Sigmund Freud's—which he meant in warning, not celebration:

> If you wish to expel religion from our European civilization you can only do it through another system of doctrines, and from the outset this would take over all the psychological characteristics of religion, the same sanctity, rigidity, and intolerance, the same prohibition of thought in self-defence.

Here is an Austrian psychoanalyst writing in German in 1927 about precisely what would manifest in America a hundred years later in the form of a book like *White Fragility* being brandished at PTA meetings, and organizations paying Ibram Kendi $20,000 for a forty-five-minute interview on Zoom. We don't use the word *religion* to describe these modern peculiarities, but note how perfectly normal they seem when we do.

Dismantling hegemonic structures?

Here, then, is the reason why, for a supposedly activist movement, the Elect so often seem rather diagonally concerned with activism. The Elect will insist that what they are doing is not founding a replacement for Protestantism, but acting upon what I have seen phrased as "an enduring white responsibility for deconstructing our own privilege and the systemic pervasiveness of white supremacy."

Ah, the seductiveness of the language.

But to forge a society in which whites are un-supreme in a fashion that would transform the experience of those trapped under the weight of the effects of institutional racism, *is it necessary* that the president and board chairman of the Poetry Foundation be forced to resign because the group's statement in allegiance with Black Lives Matter after the Floyd murder was *not long enough*?

To transform the experience of those trapped under the weight of the effects of institutional racism, *is it necessary* that when, in 2018, a woman attended a party thrown by a *Washington Post* employee and wore blackface in ridicule of a recent comment by Megyn Kelly, she was not just called aside but cast into unemployment as a revolting heretic unworthy of civilized engagement? The blackface was unwise, to be sure—by the late 2010s it was no longer within the bounds of most educated people's sense of humor to wear blackface even in irony. But still, the offender clearly intended it as signaling allegiance to the barrage of criticism against Kelly. Only in the late 2010s could this clumsy goof-up qualify as grounds for unemployment, with her callers-out claiming that she had made the party's space "unsafe," as if she had simply walked in corked up and saying she was Oprah. A few people at the party not only hounded her out but dedicated themselves to getting her fired from the newspaper for her transgression of etiquette. They succeeded, after even going as far as strong-arming the host of the party into revealing her name to them so that they could pursue her persecution.

To transform the experience of those trapped under the weight of the effects of institutional racism, *is it necessary* that when the San Francisco Museum of Modern Art was criticized for being insufficiently committed to non-white artists, and the museum's long-serving curator Gary Garrels *concurred* but added that the museum would not stop collecting white artists entirely, because this would constitute "reverse discrimination," he was fired? His use of that term was pivotal in his losing his job, for implying that non-whites, as people deprived of power, can be racist. In the 1990s, what he said in 2020 would never have left him unemployed.

The Garrels episode bears some further examination. He was fired for using a term. Meanwhile, less than a mile's walk away, in the Tenderloin of San Francisco, there cluster legions of people who can't afford housing and live their lives in makeshift tents on the street. If censuring Garrels for his lexicon has any connection to the "structures" keeping people on the streets, it's rather brutally indirect.

Yet the Elect who defenestrated Garrels speak of dismantling "structures." *Structure* is a Latinate word, with the crisp snap of the "ksh" in the middle. It sounds authoritative, especially preceded by a dramatic word like "dismantle." *Hegemony*, another word favored by the Elect, is intimidating in its way, because it's so easy to mispronounce. Deep down, you might want to pronounce it "*hedge*-a-mony," and so mastering how to really say it, and even to hear it said properly, lends a certain sense of weight.

But these are aesthetic matters. Behind these big words and menacing phrases, as often as not, is logic as sloppy as anything you might hear from a spokesperson for Donald Trump. Firing Garrels did not "function"—as these people like to use that word—to "dismantle structures," which stayed in place in the Tenderloin, a walk from the museum. Garrels's firing "functioned," as it were, to make his inquisitors feel noble, and *look* noble to one another. They were doing their duty as religious parishioners displaying their faith, not forging societal change.

It's like kiddie forts. Kids like to make forts, sometimes outdoor ones of a lean-to sort, sometimes indoor ones made out of chairs and pillows and blankets. An adult might ask just what the fort is for, and kids have their answers. If outdoors, it's to defend themselves against the neighbor kids next door—though they are actually quite friendly with those kids. If indoors, it's so they have a place where the grown-ups aren't allowed—as if the grown-ups want to bend down and get into the fort anyway, as if the kids don't have a room or rooms they can go to where the adults rarely enter except to read them bedtime stories, and as if they really want to get away from you anyway.

Kids build forts because they like building forts. As often as not, after they've built one, they don't really spend much time in it. People claiming that the "work" of white-privilege consciousness-raising is a prelude to political action are like kids pretending their forts are for protection. It feels good to say that all of this rhetoric and dismissal is necessary for changing "structures." But the real reason they are engaging in this suspiciously lengthy prelude is that there is a joy almost all of us take in hostility. Most who aren't up for wielding it themselves don't mind watching it slung.

This is human nature. You love flinging it at others partly as a balm against the pain you exert when flinging it at yourself. The guilt of the civilized, *ressentiment*: This is not just me, but Nietzsche and Freud, the humanistic canon. Wait—to be enlightened we must reject that concept as just some dead white guys sounding off? Okay, let's try this: Who doesn't get off at least a bit on squaring off and yelling "No!"? Or "Asshole!"? Or . . . *"Heretic!"*?

"How *dare* he dismiss all that we . . ." But yes, I dare to, and not only dare to, but mean it. Here's why. If Elect philosophy were really about changing the world, its parishioners would be ever champing at the bit to get out and do the changing, like Jane Addams and Dr. King.

It would be a problem among their flock: persuading adherents to sit tight and engage in the navel-gazing, set-jawed, hermetic reprogramming exercises rather than going out to do real things for real people in need. The gloomy performance art's fuzzy connection to relieving the ills of those real people in the real world would feel trivial. It would elicit disgust and dismissal from those initially attracted to something promoted as being devoted to change, until they realized it was only devoted to self-gratification.

Firing some white guy for saying "reverse discrimination" would feel like exactly what it is: kabuki. They'd want to get to the sad people huddled a skip and a jump across town on the sidewalks, and be lobbying state legislators to help them make sure no more wind up saddled with the same plight. They would be modern Dorothy Days. That is, they would be *politically active* in the fashion considered normal and urgent and laudable until recently. If those kids were really interested in defending themselves against the kids next door, they would hardly see building a little tent as a meaningful strategy.

The Elect teach us that all of this book burning and catcalling, all of these neck swivels and pliés and twerks, are necessary before getting down to actual work, but they never tell us why. Maybe the idea is that even if all of this kabuki was not necessary to get us where we are *now*, for some reason we need it to get us anywhere beyond. But that's just me trying to make some sense. Note that the Elect never present that justification, and let's face it: It'd be flabby.

Really. Teach people, by firing Garrels, to never say "reverse racism"—okay; so then, when we are safe from that term and others, San Francisco folk will rise up in the thousands and force legislators to make it so that no one ever sleeps in a tent on the sidewalk? One can only ask *What the fuck?* And no, I have caricatured not a bit. What do the Elect really intend by getting people like Garrels fired? Just how is all of their fire and brimstone—implication intended—related to the fate of actual people suffering?

"Now breathe," as Robin DiAngelo so graciously advises in her religious primer. But once we breathe, we are to fire Garrels for blaspheming—to no effect whatsoever upon a single person suffering. This is where we are.

Electism is easy.

Electism's appeal also stems from the fact that, as much as its fans claim that the relevant issues are complex, it is actually founded on aspects of cognition that are rather elemental. Electism is, ultimately, *easy.*

Example: One of the weirdest things in Robin DiAngelo's *White Fragility* is that she writes that whites think of themselves as a default category rather than as "white"—which is true—but then she often depicts whites as a frowning tribe circling the wagons and defending whiteness against threatened incursions from the brown rabble. This is a general Elect trope. You are to think of the white administrative assistant you know as someone who on the one hand doesn't understand that she is "white" but who now and then slits her eyes and votes for a white candidate for office, motivated now to defend the power of the whites she suddenly understands she is one of.

The reason for that blatant contradiction is that it is the product of the basics of human cognition. Philosopher Robert McCauley has noted, for example, that religious thought, universal to humans and less cognitively unnatural than science, tends to anthropomorphize. This explains the attraction of demonizing a "white" devil despite calling otherwise not to essentialize. The religious imperative overrides the less natural scientific one. Here is why the Elect are so comfortable sounding so much like Louis Farrakhan.

This also explains the attraction to the terms *societal racism*, *structural racism*, *systemic racism*, and *institutional racism*. All carry an implication that the battle must be against the same racism we associate with the individual bigot, "putting a face on" something otherwise forbiddingly more challenging to grapple with. For decades, Americans nationwide have quietly stubbed their toe on these terms and thought guiltily, *Isn't there a difference between an uneven playing field and prejudice?* and decided not to rock the boat by asking anyone, even themselves. The rub comes from the fact that these terms using *racism* are anthropomorphizations, of a kind driven by suspension of disbelief.

McCauley also notes that religious thought stresses agency

and simple cause-effect relationships. This explains the idea that these maleficent "whites" join hands and resist incursions on their prerogatives. Whites as a body—i.e., nationwide!—actually "do" nothing whatsoever that corresponds to this vision of them we have heard so much of in a certain hard-left strain of black intellectual rhetoric since the 1960s but now hear from white people as well. But for the Elect, reality is less important here than narrative—a hallmark of critical race "theory."

Elect language deftly straddles the gap between reality and rhetoric here with the word *function*. "X functions to keep black people mired in . . ." they say, when X is an abstraction that has no intentions and thus cannot "keep" anyone in anything. But a Latinate term like *function* does two things: (1) It implies higher reasoning in being a formal word and (2) it keeps the exact nature of the supposed thing being "done" at a distance via the abstractness of the word, because real questions seem beside the point when there is justice to be done.

Note I did not write that they simply want to deflect real questions out of some private sense of inadequacy. It is more that they feel no basic drive to dot i's and cross t's when dwelling on these matters, as they feel their orientation as indisputably correct in a fashion that dwarfs all concerns with exactness. The monsignor may muse about why God allows such suffering—and, in my experience, is given to doing so more earnestly than the Elect muse about the new religion they cherish—but ultimately, to him Jesus's grace is vastly larger than any niggling matters of getting all the ducks in a row. The Elect's heart is in battling racism and showing that they are committed to it. To them, "functions to" is enough because, after all, who killed Trayvon Martin, Michael Brown, Tamir Rice, and George Floyd? *Whites are devils, that's all that matters, and let us proselytize.*

The Elect, then, despite their general level of education and advanced vocabulary, are engaging in intuition over questioning, quietly trashing the basic orientations of scientific inquiry in favor of going back to *centering*—to use one of their favorite terms—feelings, including the atavistic kind that clamor to see people not just critiqued but punished. Michael Lind is sadly accurate in his take on the Elect, who he sees as

> reviving the preliberal, premodern religious approach to society, conceived of as a congregation of the virtuous and like-minded. Either you are a true believer or you are a heretic. There can be no compromise with wicked people, and the chief measure of wickedness is not action—[such as] engaging in overt discrimination on the basis of race—but expressing disapproved attitudes and refusing to use ritualized politically-correct language.

One of the cognitively weirdest things about the Elect is that they, despite being so articulate and so convinced that they harbor a wisdom the rest of us languish without, are ultimately more like people coming over the hill with pitchforks than the prudently informed redeemers they see themselves as.

Black people settle for Electism to feel whole.

This brings us to why black people choose to be Elect. It can't be enjoyment of the pride in sticking up for another group, because they *are* the group. Black people certainly are not virtue-signaling to one another. The condescension in Elect philosophy about black people alone would, under other conditions, leave Electism as white as QAnon, and it isn't just about Scrabble or even the cops. We're so frail we can't bear watching a white person hold one of our kids on their knee?

Consider also the idea that our main focus must ever be on smoking out remnant racist bias, with its implication that this bias is a conclusive obstacle to black success. But no such argument has ever been made for any other group in the history of the human species. We, and only we, because of something peculiar to postindustrial conditions in one nation, can truly look forward only once we have upended basic procedure. We, and only we, require a vast transformation in psychosocial and distributional procedure in what is, despite its flaws, a functioning democratic experiment in which open racism is prohibited to a degree unknown to human history before five decades ago, and to a degree that would have been considered science fiction as recently as three decades ago.

This idea paints black people as mentally and spiritually deficient children, and yet legions of black people have learned to espouse it with tearful sincerity, today often eagerly subscribing to the Catechism of Contradictions. Why do so many black people settle for it?

It can be counterintuitive that a major reason is insecurity.

It will surprise no one that a people treated like animals for centuries, under slavery, Jim Crow, and then redlining, came out with a damaged racial self-image. There is no mother country to look back upon in any real way—a black woman from Atlanta is much more like a white one than she is like a woman from Senegal. Black Americans will never occupy a separate nation of any kind to start all over again. We are all we've got, and in the 1960s something odd happened.

Segregation was outlawed, and outward racial attitudes began changing with unprecedented rapidity. In 1960 black America lived under pitiless Jim Crow, and many whites, even educated ones, barely understood when they were accused of prejudice against black people. Think of how most of the *Mad Men* characters felt, if at all, about race. By 1970 Jim Crow was gone, and educated whites, at least, were acutely aware of what racial prejudice meant, with new terms like *systemic racism* also now all but inescapable. Think of the endless ridicule of bigotry on Norman Lear sitcoms like *All in the Family* and *Maude*.

This was a wonder. It is underacknowledged today what a badge of honor this was, upon a nation we are now told is so morally irredeemable on race. However, it had an unexpected aftereffect. Segregation had been outlawed from on high, with black Americans not having had to endure the long, slow clawing our way into self-sufficiency regardless of prevailing attitudes that other groups had dealt with. In the grand scheme of things, it was a moral advance for the country that a subordinate group did not have to simply make the best of the worst with no questions asked; none of us would want to rewind the tape and play things out again without the Civil Rights Act of 1964, the Voting Rights Act of 1965, and the Fair Housing Act of 1968.

But still, this had an ironic by-product: It meant that black people could not have a basic pride in having come the whole way despite and amid unreachable dismissal and pitiless, overt roadblocks that we slowly but ultimately just pawed past and over and beyond. Driving the Civil Rights movement? This we had done, and it worked. But it was about changing the rules, and in a way, this was less useful in fostering true, gut-level, no-questions-asked pride. We could not say that we clawed our way to where we got despite whites just staying the way they were.

Black people were never as utterly shattered and "hollowed out" as Randall Robinson argued, but the reason black children chose white dolls in the famous experiment of the 1950s was a damaged racial self-image. Even black kids had already been imprinted with a subliminal idea that white was better than them. A decade-plus later, after the Civil Rights victories, the proud dissemination of slogans like Black Is Beautiful were, in their way, a symptom of the same inferiority complex. What was notable was that the very concept of black being beautiful needed to be stressed at all.

Or consider Black Power. If you went back in a time machine to about 1970 and talked to assorted black movers and shakers, you'd find little agreement as to just what that term meant, other than as a rhetorically punchy variation on Black Is

Beautiful. It was a reminder that black people could be strong—but again, the reminder was necessary, and it also pointed to little that could actually be done. It left a hole still gaping.

A people seek a substitute sense of pride and positive identity in circumstances like this. An available "hack," as we might put it today, was the status of noble victim. To all but the very most smitten fellow travelers with black people, it has always been quietly clear that much of our discourse on race entails a certain exaggeration of just how bigoted most whites are, of just how set against black achievement society has been since about 1970. Racism, in all of its facets, is real, but since the late 1960s a contingent of black thinkers has tended to insist that things were as bad as they were in 1940, leaving even many black people who actually experienced Jim Crow a tad perplexed and even put off.

There is a reason for this exaggeration. If you lack an internally generated sense of what makes you legitimate, what makes you special, then a handy substitute is the idea of yourself as a survivor. If you are insecure, a handy strategy is to point out the bad thing someone else is doing—we all remember that type from our school days—and especially if the idea is that they are doing it to *you*.

Before the late 1960s, too few white Americans would have even felt it necessary to hear black people out on this perspective. Once a critical mass of whites did, the stage was set for a sea change in what was considered "authentic" black thought. Whites—or at least a critical mass of them—now eagerly took on assuaging black grievance as a mission. This allowed a black person, if they chose, to build an identity on pointing constantly to a racism "in the air," even if the stark reality of old-school bigotry was receding quickly into the past.

What I have just outlined is couched perfectly by Shelby Steele, my first inspiration on race issues. Those who want to fully understand how so much of what frustrates us in our race dialogue is driven by insecurity can do no better than consult his *The Content of Our Character*. It's getting old now, but only in the way that wine does.

"The race thing" makes genuine sense as a religious faith.

Only in understanding this insecurity at the heart of modern black identity does the black embrace of Electism make sense from the outside. Twenty years ago, a black rapper, in an interview with a white reporter, actually came out and admitted, "I'm valid when I'm disrespected" in justifying the violence in his lyrics. That is an odd thing for any human being to say, on its face. But for many black people, pointing to being disrespected is a prime driver of their sense of purpose and self.

In 2020, after George Floyd's murder, for a while there were self-canceling strains of tweet and editorial. Some were from black people annoyed that whites were writing to them in solidarity rather than taking to the streets ("I Don't Need 'Love' Texts from My White Friends"). Some were from black people annoyed that white people were *not* writing in sympathy on social media ("Why Not Saying Anything Is Actually Saying a Lot"). The former sorts would say they wanted the people to use their feet instead of their fingers, but then the latter sorts were quite happy with just the finger support.

A white person could be pardoned for having no idea what to do here, as onlookers joyously "liked" both strains of accusation. Some see this kind of thing as black people deliberately throwing up smoke screens, but nothing so targeted was happening. Rather, unconnected people were happening upon separate ways of fulfilling the *single* Elect imperative: of having something to accuse white people of as an ersatz kind of pride. That the charges made no sense together was of no importance (more of our Catechism).

One of the people who got the woman who attended the *Washington Post* party in blackface fired said that she only started pursuing this woman's ouster afterward, rather than at the party itself, because she, a black person, felt "unsafe" doing so there. However, at this party, we can be quite sure that the other attendees felt varying degrees of sympathy with her discomfort with the face paint, and for the record this person is six foot one. It is hard to believe that she felt genuinely unsafe either physically or even socially; frankly we dishonor her by pretending she could have.

Many readers will recall times when they have seen a black person attesting to the racism they encounter while wearing a smile on their face. One forgets how odd this is. The black teen at the Black Lives Matter protest site in Seattle in 2020 who had himself recorded telling whites that black people are "holier"

---

because of the victimhood we suffer was smiling as if he was talking about how good his lunch was. It's because if noble victimhood founds your sense of self, talking of the racism you have encountered is proactive self-presentation, of a kind almost anyone would engage in with a basic life force, an enjoyment of activity, interaction, and sharing.

The sharing part is key. To be a black Elect is to have a sense of belonging. This is attractive to the white Elect as well, but it can exert an especially powerful pull when one is black. Many educated black people wrestle with a sense that they may be seen as having left their community behind, that they are not engaged in what used to be called the Struggle. One way to ease that sense of being a prodigal is to adopt an identity as a beleaguered black person, where you are united with all black people, regardless of social class or educational level, by the common experience of suffering discrimination.

But the theme here is that being Elect can be, for a black person, like a warm blanket. You belong to something. Anyone who questions how "black" you are because of your speech, appearance, interests, or upward mobility is likely to hush up if you're on the barricades with them decrying the racism of your university—or, later, your workplace, town, or country. Marx warned, in his Inaugural Address to the International Working Men's Association in 1864, of a "solidarity of defeat," where what energizes people's sense of themselves as a group is obstacles forced on them from an enemy above. Marx thought of this as a holding pattern and urged true revolution; black America can seem oddly stuck in almost brandishing the defeat as a badge of pride. But this is understandable as a kind of therapy. Humans seek pride where they can get it.

It must be clear, then, that much of what can seem confusing about many black people's take on racism is due not to manipulativeness but to filling a hole, in a way all humans seek to in assorted ways. Black people who insist that black America can do no better than okay until racist sentiments no longer exist, societal procedures yield no racial disparities, and all Americans can perform a lengthy recitation on black social history are fixing themselves. Their alienation is therapeutic.

Black Electness is old school.

The pathway is short, then, between critical race theory's celebration of communal "narrative" over empirical truth and this modern black frame of mind in which exaggeration is allowed to pass as a kind of alternate form of honesty. In fact, in black America the seeds for it were planted even earlier.

Many readers may have noticed that the kind of ideology I am addressing hardly began in 2020, or even 2010 or 1990, and has been especially familiar from a certain segment of black people for a very long time. It was in the 1960s and '70s that it became default among black intellectuals to seek not just the social but the psychological transformation of America, a fraught and largely fruitless mission whose results were less important than its affording an ongoing reason to wax pessimistic.

Here's a bit of an actual encounter group session from about

1970 in which a black psychiatrist named Cobbs squares off against a white woman:

> WOMAN: I don't relate towards you, towards color or anything else, I relate towards every single person here as an individual.
>
> COBBS: You're lying, you're lying, you're lying!
>
> WOMAN: Why?
>
> COBBS: If I would say "you look like a little boy to me, I just don't see anything" you'd say I was crazy because you're a woman. . . . If I could neutralize you in some way this is exactly what white folks do to black folks.

Many will recognize this as what became precisely the "racial healing" in the sessions Robin DiAngelo espouses in *White Fragility*. The construct predated her by a long shot, and it was as performative and useless then as it is now.

Sessions like that illustrate that among black people, the Elect kind of thought has been established among many for a very long time. What distinguishes our era is the number of white people who have taken up the politics of black radicalism since about 2013, and especially since 2020. To wit: The essence of the Elect's new moment is a critical mass of white people coming to think like a charismatic hard-left contingent of black people have been thinking for decades.

Some black people's response will be that America listens to the truth only when white people take it up. But that's just it: What's being taken up is *not* "truth." The hard-left, endlessly pessimistic take on race among a certain gorgeously countercultural contingent of black people, who started with dashikis and now sit in faculty meetings demanding that their colleagues testify to their racism, has always been longer on showbiz than results. For all of the fascination it exerts, black America's gains since the 1960s have happened in spite of, not because of, black radicalism. Whites are now taking up the same banner in our names—but who among us will say that whites' participation proves that a black agenda is truth?

Thus, when Representative Ayanna Pressley casually says, "If you're not prepared to come to the table and represent that voice, don't come, because we don't need any more brown faces that don't want to be a brown voice. We don't need black faces that don't want to be a black voice," she probably isn't thinking about Richard Delgado and Regina Austin. She's saying something that legions of black people would have applauded long before critical race theory even existed. She means a general idea that being oppressed by white racism defines the black American condition, experienced by all of us to a crushing degree, such that to deny or even downplay it can only be read as dishonest, and therefore inauthentic. Stokely Carmichael and Eldridge Cleaver were as comfortable with that kind of view fifty years ago as Pressley is now. The difference today is that so many whites now think of this view not as defeatist oversimplification from certain black radicals, but as truth they are morally bound to evangelize.

When anyone questions this Manichaean take on racism in modern America, the Elect black person often responds with white-hot fury. That has been the case since about 1966, and leaves onlookers wondering why this infuriated person is so impatient with differing views. This misses the essence of the matter. The fury is that of someone who feels one's entire sense of purpose and legitimacy as a human being is under interrogation and threat. This response is not confusing in the least when we perceive its religious nature.

Other ways of being black.

If we seek an anthropological kind of analysis of where our society is at this point, we must understand that this Elect frame of mind is not universal among black people, or even dominant beyond the highly educated.

For example, a Pew Research Center survey identified something readily apparent on the ground: that college often teaches black students a view of whites as oppressors. Nine percent of black high-school students report experiencing racism regularly; the number doubles among black college graduates, to 17.5 percent.

We are trained to think, upon reading that, that black students undergo racist experiences in college that they hadn't had before, or that black high-school students are missing aspects of discrimination that maturity makes clearer. This is a reasonable response, but it doesn't really go through. So often we are told that even black adolescents and teens are undergoing racist slights and underestimations on a regular basis. As in: If I were to say that black adolescents and teens do *not* undergo racist slights and underestimations on a regular basis, a great many people would be quite outraged.

Even the polling data suggest that the issue is more what one has been taught to say than what one actually feels. Half of black people with college degrees say that racism has made them fear for their safety; just a third of younger black students do. But why would college put black people in more physical danger from racists or racism? Any story about cops profiling college students is a tragedy—but who will say that the same thing doesn't happen to teenagers? Many of us can list some names.

Yet, especially these days, it will be difficult for many people to imagine that there is, or has ever been, a "black" way of thinking other than that of Ta-Nehisi Coates and Ayanna Pressley. It may seem to confer a certain legitimacy on the white Elect, the idea being that all black people except the occasional quisling have always thought this way, and whites evidence moral advancement in joining us at last.

But while Elect thought goes a ways back with black people, it has never been anything close to universal. A neat illustration is a 1971 episode of *All in the Family*, created at a time when one can be pardoned for supposing that all black thought paralleled that of Angela Davis and Amiri Baraka.

Two young black men break into Archie's house, and "knee-jerk liberal" son-in-law Mike warmly tells them that he understands that they are doing this because of the hopeless conditions they grew up in. The burglars actually laugh at this and feel diminished by it, sensing themselves as more complex individuals than that. It bears mentioning that one of them is played by

Cleavon Little, with the same serenely one-step-ahead-of-y'all demeanor he infused his signature *Blazing Saddles* role with a few years later. In other words, the burglars' take is portrayed as the sophisticated one.

So much for the idea that black lawbreaking will teach white people a lesson and that the black condition is summed up by oppression. And this episode was written by whites who considered themselves enlightened about "the race thing," something that the show's creator, Norman Lear, considered a defining commitment. That this episode's premise would feel like an alternate universe in a Spike Lee movie today is evidence that progressivism manifests itself differently according to era. We must contrast that *All in the Family* episode with a routine familiar to any New York subway rider today: black boys peddling candy and noting, "We're just trying to keep out of trouble," as if it is inevitable that trouble would find them if they weren't engaged in (illegal) commerce underground.

Okay, the *All in the Family* episode was created by whites; the burglars were fictional characters. But they reflected how many black people thought back in the day, in no way considering it cosmically inevitable and pardonable that black people underperform and commit crimes because the playing field isn't level. In 1957, an episode of the television documentary series *See It Now* covered segregation and its damage to black lives. A black letter writer sent in a letter complaining that the episode had not shown "the many of our race who are on top." To this person, the idea of keeping black success under wraps out of a quest to keep whites guilty made no sense—and anyone who wants to say that the letter writer was naive must remember that they grew up in Jim Crow America.

Similarly, in the 1950s, black leaders criticized the minstrel-esque television sitcom *Amos 'n Andy* for not showing enough successful black people—as opposed to fifteen years later, when a new generation of black writers roasted the sitcom *Julia*, about a middle-class nurse, for not showing *enough* poverty and racism! These critics were the new black Elect. The ones who had protested *Amos 'n Andy* had known an America where lynching was regular, and yet to the new bunch, the old guard's interest in seeing black success on television was naive.

In 1966, the Detroit branch of the National Urban League distributed little theatrical sketches showing how inner-city kids could get jobs more easily. In one, "Mo," who says "Uh-huh" and "Naw, man," and dresses how he wants to, doesn't get the job; he gets one when he uses standard English with the interviewer and dresses professionally. Today, the Elect cringe at the idea of a black kid being made to conform to the ways of the oppressor, but in 1966 that would have been a back-of-the-room opinion held by only a few. Yet what would justify saying that the Elect take on "Mo" is an advance? What alternate employment strategies are they proposing?

A more random example: I am deeply fond of comedian Cristela Alonzo. Her short-lived sitcom *Cristela* was a joy forever—I would have followed it for ten seasons. In her 2017 television comedy special, she now and then recounts racist assumptions against Latinos, and wears an expression that says "What the . . . ?" Every time she flashes that expression, it occurs to me that the Elect kind of black person is odder than they suppose in not being able to harbor that dismissive expression about casual racism. To them, their job is to shout to the heavens all minor matters of overgeneralizing and clumsiness as evidence of moral perversion requiring the excommunication of anyone who was responsible for it.

If Cristela can do it, why not us? She is being a psychologically healthy person; Elect catechism teaches us that we are ahead of the curve to be psychologically broken. The notion that real blackness means framing casual racism as close to physical abuse is a modern one. It feels right only to people who, deep down, do not feel right at all.

THE SELLOUT CHARGE EXPLAINED

A common accusation is that black thinkers who question the Elect orthodoxy are traitorous Judases out to make a buck. The assumption is that there exist black people who decide to go against their actual opinions—which simply *must* be the Elect's, since *living while black* is such an unmitigated tragedy—and cater to what right-wing whites want to hear.

I presume that the detractors do not assume that such people actually harbor their opinions honestly, because this would entail that it is somehow immoral for black people who honestly do not think like Ta-Nehisi Coates to air their views in public. That would make no sense at all, and I assume the detractors are sensible people. As such, they must think that black conservatives are dishonest.

But I have met a considerable number and range of black people right of center, and I have never met a single one who fit the "Uncle Tom" description. Or, if any of them were, they hid it with a deftness that actually only a trained and gifted actor could pull off. The Judas slur is just that. It has no basis in reality. And really, has anyone ever actually thought there were such people? Who would marry such a person? How could such people live with themselves? How common are actual monsters?

Yet there are many black people given to labeling black people who disagree with them on race issues as cartoon villains *they could not sincerely think the people are.* We are once again in religion's territory. Written history, and even retained historical memory, confirms that seismic sociohistorical change can happen via protest and agitation, but without kangaroo court inquisitions, without psychological torture sessions seeking to purge people of improper thoughts, without obsessive policing of language. This empirical, intuitive reality matters not to our parishioners, because they have become accustomed to a subconscious rerouting of reasoning on a certain realm of existence, due to its attractions for reasons beyond the sociopolitical.

This explains why even centrist views on race are so often tarred as "selling out." The logical sloppiness of it comes from a kind of desperation, born of a basic sense of personal injury. The guiding commandment is that we battle power differentials, especially racism, via spreading the Word. The black conservative wants to improve black lives just as they do but refuses to join their particular battle. The black conservative sees battling "racism" as futile, and seeks alternate ways of helping people make the best of themselves. As such, they counter the Word. That, from the Elect perspective, is not "a different view," but heresy. Heresy makes you mad.

4

WHAT'S WRONG WITH IT BEING A RELIGION? IT HURTS BLACK PEOPLE.

ONE RESPONSE TO A book like this might be to own that Electism is a religion. You might consider it a better one than, say, believing that God's son died for our sins and was reborn, waiting to envelop you in his eternal grace if you believe in him. This new religion is about countering racism. Who could be against that?

But we must ask whether the Elect approach actually shows signs of making any difference in the lives of black people, other than by making educated white people infantilize them. While purportedly "dismantling racist structures," the Elect religion is actually harming the people living in those structures. It is a terrifyingly damaging business. Here is how Elect ideology does not genuinely care about the welfare of black people.

You are to turn a blind eye to black kids getting jumped by other ones in school.

You are to turn a blind eye to black undergraduates cast into schools where they are in over their heads, and into law schools incapable of adjusting to their level of preparation in a way that will allow them to pass the bar exam.

You are to turn a blind eye to the willful dimness of condemning dead people for moral lapses normal in their time, as if they were still alive.

You are to turn a blind eye to the folly in the idea of black "identity" as all about what whites think rather than about what black people themselves think.

You are to turn a blind eye to lapses in black intellectuals' work, because black people lack white privilege.

You are to turn a blind eye to the fact that social history is complex, and instead pretend that those who tell you that all racial discrepancies are a result of racism are evidencing brilliance.

You are to turn a blind eye to innocent children taught to think in these ways practically before they can hold a pencil.

Let's take a tour of what the Elect require you to think about black people.

The Elect on school discipline: The bigotry against black boys.

Black boys get suspended and expelled from schools more than other kids. According to Elect ideology, this must be because they are discriminated against.

Specifically, we are told to think that the reason these boys get disciplined more than other kids is because teachers hold biases against them. The white kid acting up is a scamp; the black kid acting up is a thug. There are scholar-activists who have founded whole careers on bringing this wisdom to America's educators and beyond. In 2014, a "Dear Colleague" letter went out from the U.S. Department of Education concurring that black boys are disciplined disproportionately because of racism. In 2019, the U.S. Commission on Civil Rights released a briefing report making the same case, titled "Beyond Suspensions: Examining School Discipline Policies and Connections to the School-to-Prison Pipeline for Students of Color with Disabilities."

Noble notions from noble entities. But the simple fact is this: Black boys do commit more violent offenses in public schools than other kids. Period. The Elect earnestly decry that most black kids go to school with only other black kids, because it fits into their agenda to point out "segregation." But that "segregation" also entails that the black boys they think should be allowed to beat up other kids in school are handing out the beatings *to other black kids*. This means that if we follow these prophets' advice and go easier on black boys, we hinder the education of other black students.

For example, *The Philadelphia Inquirer* fanned out across the city's public schools in 2012 and found that there had been thirty thousand violent incidents in public schools between 2007 and then, which included robberies, rapes, and a pregnant teacher punched in the stomach. (She was one of four thousand teachers assaulted by students between 2005 and 2010.)

Out of the desire not to stereotype black kids, one might interpret those numbers in various ways designed to take the focus off of black boys. However, these interpretations just don't work out.

For example, one might imagine that a lot of these assaults may have been committed by white kids. But the numbers don't square with it: In Philadelphia's public schools, more than two in three students (70 percent) are black or Latino.

Or one might imagine that, just maybe, those white kids who make up one-third of the students are committing a disproportionate amount of the assaults? But other studies reveal that black boys are responsible for a disproportionate amount of school violence. The National Center for Education Statistics found that in 2015, 12.6 percent of black kids surveyed nationwide had had a fight on school grounds, while only 5.6 percent of white kids had. It was not a fluke year: In 2013, the numbers were 12.8 percent vs. 6.4. In other words, black kids were more than twice as likely to engage in violence at school as white kids.

A Fordham Institute study showed the same thing in 2019. It surveyed twelve hundred black and white elementary and high school teachers nationwide and found that teachers in high-poverty schools were twice as likely as those in other schools to say that verbal disrespect was a daily occurrence in their classrooms, six times as likely to say that physical fighting was a daily or weekly occurrence, and three times as likely to report being personally assaulted by a student. One might ask, to be sure, whether high-poverty schools are always predominantly black or Latino ones—and the answer is that they usually are. The Elect endlessly teach us that brown people are disproportionately poor in America, and if this report had been about hunger or lead paint, they would readily accept it as largely referring to brown kids. It would be inconsistent to suddenly read the Fordham Institute study through a studiously deracialized lens.

In fact, the teachers in this study often reported that in the wake of calls like the ones above to treat disciplining black boys as bigotry, underreporting of serious incidents was "rampant," and also that higher tolerance for misbehavior was in part responsible for the recent decline in student suspensions.

Reports from a New York City initiative have even more explicitly located an especial problem with school violence among black boys. The initiative sought to reduce suspensions of black boys in response to the reports claiming that the suspensions were driven by racism. Teachers reported less order and discipline in their classrooms, *particularly in black- and Latino-dominated secondary schools.* Many black teachers said that suspensions and similar kinds of discipline should be used *more* often, despite the fact that black teachers were slightly more likely to believe also that school discipline could be racially biased. In the high-poverty schools, 60 percent of African American teachers—slightly *more* than the 57 percent of white teachers—said that issues with student behavior made learning difficult.

Those are the facts. You must consider them the next time you see an earnest, probably black or Latino person in business clothes claiming that "black boys" get a raw deal in disciplining. If they can't defend themselves in view of the studies mentioned above, or give no evidence of having even learned of them, they are not teaching but preaching, and for a purpose that leaves legions of black and Latino kids not only improperly educated but beaten up. Note: I have spared you the accounts of physical assault these kids' teachers often suffer as well.

The Elect will see only "racism" here, but only because their religious commitment numbs them to the harm their view does to real children living their lives in the real world. Obviously, poverty can make kids more likely to be violent—there is no reason to see these boys as pathological beings. But to insist that bigotry is the only possible reason for suspending more black boys than white boys is to espouse harming black students.

The Elect on university admissions: Yale or jail.

It's often thought that affirmative action at universities involves, simply, considering racial diversity only after assembling a pool of students with the same caliber of grades and test scores. The vision is that all candidates have the same scores, and then you fill out a certain pie chart. Few reasonable people would have a problem with that kind of system, even if the brown students are just a touch lower in scores, at which point there is what we could call a thumb on the scale. Just a thumb.

But the question is whether black and Latino students should be admitted with *significantly* lower grades and test scores than those that would admit a white or Asian student. This is how racial preferences in university admissions have traditionally worked, especially beyond a few tippy-top schools such as the one I teach at, and there is no question that it has been common. It was most widely aired during the *Gratz v. Bollinger* case against the University of Michigan in the early 2000s, where it was revealed that being black alone gave applicants twenty out of the one hundred points necessary for admission, but this was one of many such cases that have been discovered nationwide. This means that there is what has been called a "mismatch" between students' dossiers and the schools they are admitted to.

Many insist that despite the initial mismatch, the students excel nevertheless and the mismatch has no actual effect. But this would mean that the admissions standards applied to other students are meaningless, and actual studies have shown, not surprisingly, that this is not the case. At Duke University, economist Peter Arcidiacono, with Esteban Aucejo and Joseph Hotz, has shown that the "mismatch" lowers the number of black scientists. Black students at a school where teaching is faster and assumes more background than they have often leave a major in frustration, but would be less likely to have done so at a school prepared to instruct them more carefully.

In 2004, UCLA law professor Richard Sander revealed an especially tragic tendency in this vein, showing that "mismatched" law students are much more likely to cluster in the bottom of their classes and, especially, to fail the bar exam. Predictably, the study attracted much criticism, but no one has refuted its basic observations, as opposed to fashioning reasons why they should for some reason not concern us. It is similarly unlikely that anyone could tell Arcidiacono, Aucejo, and Hotz that what they chronicled was mirages.

That students thrive at different paces is hardly rocket science. Because of the societal factors that dismay us all—quality of schooling, parents denied good education themselves, complex home lives—black and Latino students are often less prepared for how quickly students are expected to take in information at selective schools. But the question is: Do we respond to this by nonetheless placing them in schools teaching over their heads?

Plato's *Republic* runs about three hundred pages. At Columbia, we assign it as the first reading of the year in the Contemporary Civilization class all sophomores must take. They are expected to have been able to get through it, to discuss it for two or three two-hour classes, and to refer to it in a paper or two after that, not to mention retain familiarity with it some weeks later for the midterm. Imagine being a student who is quite bright but is from a home without many books in it. He isn't the fastest reader in the world, and his schools didn't expose him to much discussion of disembodied ideas as opposed to matters relevant to daily life. All of a sudden, he's in a classroom where students marinated since toddlerhood in books and top-quality education are confidently discussing this book, blithely tossing off concepts he's barely heard of, all doing a fine job of at least faking having gotten through all three hundred pages.

Now imagine this student at a school where about forty pages of the *Republic* are assigned, likely including the passage about the cave, with the professor making sure to usher students through the contours of the argument, aware that most of them have rarely engaged a text of this kind. Which class is this student going to be most comfortable in, and in which class are they likely to get a better grade on their paper? And given that, regardless of education level, nobody remembers much about three hundred whole pages four years later, has this student really gotten a raw deal in terms of education? Some Columbia students would be quite happy if we assigned only forty pages and went over them with a fine-tooth comb.

Yet the discussion of affirmative action implies that the choice is somehow between Yale or jail, as if the few dozen highly selective universities were the only ticket to lifetime success. But here's what happens on the ground. At the University of California, San Diego, the year before racial preferences were banned in the late 1990s, exactly one black student out of 3,268 freshmen made honors. A few years later, after students who once would have been "mismatched" to Berkeley or UCLA were being admitted to schools like UC San Diego, one in five black freshmen at the latter school were making honors, the same proportion as white ones.

There is a reason few have ever heard about things like that. The ban on racial preferences at University of California schools elicited Proto-Electness 101, with endless oratory about how the ban meant that kids from poor black neighborhoods would be "denied education," as if Berkeley and UCLA were the only schools available. Supposedly a Berkeley would revert to "segregation," with the implication that, privately, this is what white people running the place really wanted.

Never mind that this "segregated" Berkeley never happened.

That black kids were not being consigned to eventual unemployment by attending UC Santa Cruz instead was not discussed. The guiding impulse was to cry racism, reason be damned. It was critical race theory in action. The Proto-Elect of the time accepted the tacit idea that to apply reason as opposed to emotion to the issues was unsporting, too "white." That we needed to make it so that more black kids truly qualified for Berkeley and UCLA was considered a sideline point, while it was also in the air that for black kids to perform at that level was a little suspicious, as if they had given in to the "white" ethos too fully.

If that sounds impressionistic, I taught at Berkeley back then, and must note that after the ban was put in place, a black undergraduate told me, outright, that she and others working at the minority recruitment office were afraid that black students admitted without racial preferences would not be interested in being part of a black community at the school. It was the baldest affirmation of the idea that being a nerd isn't authentically black that I have ever heard: May 1998, circa 4 o'clock on a weekday afternoon.

It is sentiments of that kind that condition people to fight for exempting black students from the level of competition other kids have to deal with regardless of their background. It is also self-involved white guilt and its lack of genuine concern for black people's fate. The data on the calamities the mismatch policy creates are now overwhelming, and yet are indignantly swatted away because they are not consonant with announcing one's awareness that racism exists. The result: black undergraduates and law students in over their heads nationwide while an influential cadre of people intone lines about "dismantling structures."

The Elect on the quality of black minds: Condescension as respect.

In *Between the World and Me*, required reading for millions of undergraduates nationwide for years now, Ta-Nehisi Coates states that he had no sympathy for the white cops and firemen who died at the World Trade Center on 9/11. They were just "menaces of nature; they were the fire, the comet, the storm, which could—with no justification—shatter my body."

Good writing. But Coates wrote this of people with families. Spouses, and especially children, never saw Daddy again. Even in view of the relationship between cops and black men, which surely informed this pitilessness in Coates, the numbness to personal grief, the dehumanization of the family members those people left behind amid a titanic and unusual tragedy, was stunningly cold. It was unexamined and irresponsible for someone billed as a public intellectual.

Yet the white punditocracy at most tsk-tsked him for it. In our society, where a person can be roasted as a moral pervert and fired for wearing blackface makeup as a joke (the *Washington Post* employee) or for *criticizing one and a half Asian celebrities while white* (Alison Roman), Coates was allowed to say that those white public servants deserved to die but continued to be celebrated as America's lead prophet on race.

The only reason Coates was given this pass was condescension: brute denigration (word chosen deliberately) of a black human being. To not hold Coates responsible for the horror of a judgment like that—imagine it coming from, for example, John Lewis—and to even assign the book containing it to impressionable young people nationwide is to treat him as someone not responsible for his actions. It is to treat Coates as a child. He is being patted on the head the way Benny Hill did to bald little Jackie Wright. *Pat-a-pat-pat, you're cute.*

Black journalist Nikole Hannah-Jones insists that the Revolutionary War was fought to preserve slavery. She got a Pulitzer for it. The 1619 Project included more, indeed, but the claim about the Revolutionary War and the resultant redating of America's birth to 1619, when slavery can be argued to have begun, was the main thing that attracted so much attention to it. Hannah-Jones would have won no prize for a series without that central claim.

An enlightened America is supposed to hold a public figure accountable for her ideas. On the issue of the Revolutionary War, Hannah-Jones's claim is quite simply false, but our current cultural etiquette requires pretending that isn't true—because she is black. Someone has received a Pulitzer Prize for a mistaken interpretation of historical documents about which legions of actual scholars are expert. Meanwhile, the claim is being broadcast, unquestioned, in educational materials being distributed across the nation.

Few things suggest the encroaching penetration of the Elect into the gray matter of this country more than the breezy acceptance by so many of this utter diminishment of Hannah-Jones. White people patting her on the head for being "brave" or "getting her views out there," rather than regretting that she slipped up and wishing her better luck next time, are bigots of a kind. They are condescending to a black woman who deserves better, even if the zeitgeist she has been minted in prevents her from knowing it herself.

Racist, too, are those who actually hear out black scientists claiming that the reason there are so few black physicists is "racism." Unless these people point out black scientists doing the same work of the same caliber as their white colleagues and being refused PhDs or postdoctoral fellowships or jobs, they are out of court. If the claim is not that the "racism" is of this overt kind, then it must be the institutional racism that affects people before college. But allowing that point, what kind of sense is there in indicting universities and research labs for it, as if they can address the inadequate science teaching in public schools in black neighborhoods? To not ask this of these complainants directly, and require a real answer, may feel like a kind of courtesy, but it is actually patronization.

And as for the proposal that, say, physics needs to change what is considered real work so that a "black" perspective is allowed, to even allow this at the table is more condescension. Presumably the "alternate" perspective would eschew the tough, uncompromising higher mathematics that the serious physicist is supposed to command. Surely the idea isn't that black physicists will command the math but do it "blackly" or "diversely."

If I sound rhetorical, consult an interesting paper by black physicist Chanda Prescod-Weinstein, in which she condemns "white empiricism" as keeping black women out of physics. You will work to glean what she considers a viable alternative, but it is clear that she thinks reasoning from A to B to C is just one way of being a scientist. So we must cultivate a cadre of physicists without real chops so that STEM isn't "so white." Never mind that when other physicists cannot help but treat these "diverse" physicists as lesser achievers in subtle ways, there will be more reason to cry racism.

That's just thinking too far ahead. The imperative is to be able to identify racism and have white people nod sagely that physics is racistly biased against brown faces and needs to "address" it. This is yet more treating black people like dolts in the name of something called decentering whiteness. Moreover, to address these things in this way is to not "get it." But actually, what there is to "get" is that this is religious thought, which allows guiding commitments that do not make worldly sense.

In other words, if to be black is really to spend all of life running up against racism, as often as not that racism is in the form of this kind of patronizing dismissal. The KIPP academies, a charter school network devoted to giving poor brown kids a solid education and getting them into college, have decided that they've been too hard on the children. Their sin: the slogan "Work hard. Be nice."

KIPP has announced that to expose their charges to that mantra "diminishes the significant effort to dismantle systemic racism, places value on being compliant and submissive, supports the illusion of meritocracy, and does not align with our vision of students being free to create the future they want."

Translation: Schools committed to helping kids make the best of a bad hand now feel uncomfortable teaching their students that following rules and putting forth effort will have beneficial results. Rather, there are apparently other, woker pathways to creating a successful future, as in the "future they want." Apparently this is a future you can have without following rules, while distrusting effort as playing the white man's game.

The KIPP people are suspending common sense as well as true compassion, in a fashion that their teachers would never consider for their own children at home. This is the Elect at work, espousing a charismatic but senseless dogma as a public posture of moral goodness. Their religion supplants earlier ones in which, rather often, "Work hard. Be nice" would have qualified as wisdom. The Elect's mantra instead is *Battle racism, be indignant*—even at the expense of the well-being of black American people, including black children.

The Elect on identity: Black people's essence is not being white.

I once was having trouble understanding why a certain collection of essays by a person of color quite held together as a unitary presentation, as a whole "book."

Someone else assigned to evaluate the same book contributed that he thought it was coherent in that the essays were all about "identity."

The person intoned *identity* with a quietly warm expression, as if he had said "family" or "blueberry muffins." And for assorted people in the room, that word alone was suasional. As a theme, "identity" was as compelling to them as "climate change" would have been.

But one might ask: Just why did they consider "identity" so crucial a theme for a collection of otherwise disparate essays? In 1950, no one would have cited such a thing, whether termed "identity" or some other word, as rendering a book worthy of a prize. What, actually, did the man even mean by "identity"?

When the Elect, taking a cue from a usage that emerged among academics in the humanities and social sciences, say "identity," they are referring to how a non-white person processes their not being white and their relationship to white people's oppression.

Electism calls for everyone who isn't white to found their primary sense of self on *not being white and knowing whites don't quite "get" me.* Electism forbids us non-whites from being individual selves, out of an idea that white racism is so onerous that our self-definition must be fashioned against it, despite that this vastly exaggerates the role of racism in most black lives— including that *police brutality, while appalling, is just one of thousands of types of experience one goes through from cradle to grave, if at all.* Your Elect friend may claim that I am distorting what they believe. Ask them to specify just how it does so—and the word-salad answer they craft while looking over your shoulder will show you that I am not.

Here is where wokeness takes us back to the balkanized and artificial racial categorizations we all thought we wanted to get past. Yet ask why we are no longer supposed to get past them and the Elect—wait for it—suspect you of white supremacy. All of the Enlightenment's focus on individualism, all of modernism's permission for people to be themselves rather than live bound to preset classifications, falls to pieces before this idea that to be anything but white requires obsession with the fact that you are *not* white, and diminished by their *possibly* not seeing you in your totality.

Let us specify: Under the Elect, blackness becomes what you *aren't*—i.e., seen fully by whites—as opposed to what you *are.* It is what someone *does* to you, rather than what you *like to do.* And all of this is thought of as advanced rather than backward thought. All "because racism." Racism *über alles,* but the problem is that Elect philosophy teaches black people to live obsessed with just how someone maybe doesn't quite fully like them, and then die unappeased.

This is the meaning of life? This is the grand answer that philosophy has been seeking for millennia? But educated whites clap back at the idea that the essence of being black is how whites don't see you, as in *New York Times* film critic A. O. Scott iconically writing that "racism is what makes us white."

. . .

A SAD MANY PEOPLE fail to understand that this studiously "antiracist" conception of black identity invalidates calls for people to stress their individuality. Roughly, the idea is this: Because of what happened to George Floyd, the wise black person must think of their primary defining trait as being someone who could suffer Floyd's fate.

For example, black philosopher Kwame Anthony Appiah has written widely and artfully about the value of individualism over simplistic balkanized "identities." However, under the Elect zeitgeist, Appiah is wrong. This Ghanaian British gay man is to perceive himself primarily, and we are to perceive him primarily, as "a black man" just like Chris Rock, Samuel Jackson, Michael Brown, Trayvon Martin, and George Floyd, despite that he has nothing meaningful in common with any of them. We are to fashion this caricatured sense of him mainly because he is a touch more likely than Steven Pinker to have trouble with cops.

As such, it is missing the point to think, as many do, that Elect ideology simply recapitulates the essentialism of bygone figures like Johann Gottfried von Herder and his sense of people as divisible into "nationalities" of distinct "spirits." The Elect are not arbitrarily dividing people into classes such as Hungarians and Swedes. There is a power differential slashing through the groups they perceive. They are distinguishing whites from those whom whites oppress, with the idea that *being oppressed* is an essence in itself. It isn't about the horizontality of, say,

Teutonic essence in contrast to Slavic essence, but the verticality of *who is hurting who.*

The problem here is not only that of how black people are urged to conceive of themselves, but what they are even to consider interesting, what they are to engage in during the short time on earth during which any human lives. When "identity"—i.e., against the white hegemon—is thought of as central to intellectual, aesthetic, and moral significance, one's range of interests inevitably narrows. As such, Electness discourages genuine curiosity.

HERE IS WHERE WE GET, for example, the tacit idea that any book a black American person writes must be centered on race, racism, or battling racism. I ask the reader: Name a *nonfiction* book by a black American writer that neither battles nor even addresses race or racism.

As someone reading this book, you may know that I have written some. But can you name others? And then I will turn the screws just a bit more and ask whether you can name one by anyone beyond Neil DeGrasse Tyson and Thomas Sowell. (Malcolm Gladwell grew up in Canada.) And it is no accident that Sowell and I are both known for our resistance to a certain orthodoxy on race.

I know there are some black nonfiction writers out there of more conventional politics on race who write without being "race men (people)." But the fact that the ones most readers could name are such a small set is indicative—namely, of the tacit sense among black American writers *as well as our white supporters* that our job is to write only in service to the Struggle. We are to write on the basis of our fundamental "identity" as victims of whiteness, and if we don't, we don't know "who we are" and have done the race a disservice in being asleep at the switch. That assumption regularly drives who the (white) publishing industry gives decent book advances to, and that has only become more the case since 2020.

Zora Neale Hurston in 1938 asked, "Can the black poet sing a song to the morning?" and noted that, no, "the one subject for a Negro is the Race and its sufferings and so the song of the morning must be choked back. I will write of a lynching instead." Nothing has changed since 1938 except that if you read that passage aloud, a squad of undergraduates might report you to the diversity coordinator because it includes the word *Negro*. And of course, today we must write not of a lynching per se but of what happened to George Floyd, and the societal attitudes that led to it.

I have a personal example. We writers all have our dud books (*All About the Beat*, anyone?), but my *Talking Back, Talking Black*, about why Black English is legitimate speech, was not one of them. Overall, people seemed to like it. But Jamil Smith, a black journalist, was an exception.

Reviewing it in *The New York Times*, he didn't like that I hadn't devoted the book to the role that racism plays in how we hear the dialect. I mentioned it here and there, but the book's main strategy was to simply show how complicated, vast, and fierce the dialect is. I wasn't interested in spending 150 pages just tsk-tsking white people, and am always perplexed that so many black writers are content with spending their careers doing little but that. The subject of Black English lends itself to more, and as a human being of normal curiosity, I sought to embrace the more.

But because the book wasn't mainly about making white people uncomfortable, for Smith it was unsatisfying. People said to me at the time that he seemed to have wanted me to write a different book. That was dead-on, and note just what kind of book he would have preferred. Smith is typical of Elect black thinkers in assuming—so deeply that he does not even know it is an assumption—that describing, debating, and decrying racism must be black people's main goal in communicating with the public. To this kind of person, reading a book on Black English that isn't about telling white people they are racists in every second paragraph is like listening to a drummer who can't quite keep the beat. Something is off—there's a job not getting done. Smith thought I was mistaken in, as it were, not writing of a lynching.

ALSO RELEVANT IS THE DRUMBEAT of abuse from many black people against my friend Thomas Chatterton Williams, a black writer with a white (and French) wife whose two sons are so light-skinned that the idea of terming them "black" seems rather abstract. Williams has written insightfully that, especially today, we need to reconsider the idea that a person with any small biological component of African must "identify" as black.

When a biracial person who is half white and half black says they "aren't black," the classic objection is that they will be *seen* as black and must therefore refrain from any notion that they won't suffer discrimination. But what about when they are so light in color that no one would read them as black and would just guess that they are something other than 100 percent white?

If the person phenotypically could be anything from Latino to half Asian to Filipino to whatever—an increasingly common thing in the twenty-first century—then the next objection from the Elect is that being anything *but* white subjects you to racism analogous to that experienced by black Americans. But is it true that being a "BIPOC" of any kind subjects one to a kind of one-size-fits-all discrimination? Will the unspecifiably half-X and half-Y person be denied jobs? Will they be socially marginalized if they seek white company or even romance? Will the cops think of them as threats? And if they aren't, then just why, we must ask, must they "identify" as black, unless to join the ranks of the black Elect in savoring the comfort zone of hating whiteness rather than loving themselves?

I will never forget giving a talk at a university where a persistent questioner was an undergraduate who was half white and half Asian. She looked either white or white plus a touch of something unidentifiable. Back in the day, she could have easily "passed" as white. But, in line with our current zeitgeist, she was deeply immersed in a sense of herself as oppressed by racism. She especially decried that people expected her to be smart because of her "Asianness"—even though that Asianness was only vaguely perceptible from her appearance—and she couldn't quite square herself with my gentle response that I could not see her as oppressed in a way she needed to define herself on the basis of.

She was essentially Thomas Chatterton Williams's child grown up, except half Asian instead of half black. This woman was adopting a sense of existential grievance that her daily experiences did not justify. Being assumed to be smart can be something of a nuisance, I'm sure, but it is not exactly what most would consider suffering from the depredations of the Man.

It follows easily that we need to start reconsidering our sense of racial classifications. Namely, if we really believe that race is a fiction, we need to let racially indeterminate people make the case for that, by letting go of the idea that anyone with one peep of non-whiteness in them must "identify" as not white. We must ask why someone who doesn't even appear black must "own" their blackness in the twenty-first century *in the way Jefferson Davis and Bull Connor would have preferred them to*. Who can't see, on at least some level, the basic nonsensicality in this requirement—including that even what happened to George Floyd does not somehow justify it?

Yet for arguing this in the public sphere, Williams is often roasted as a race traitor by people sincerely thinking of themselves as bearers of a progressive message. Ladies and gentlemen, this is the Elect.

IN SUM, on the question of "identity," Elect ideology requires non-white people to found their sense of self on not being white, and on not liking how white people may or may not feel about them. No one would wish this self-conception on their child when laid out explicitly in this way. The idea of it as progressive is false. It sits as a gloomy, illogical, and pointless burden upon the souls of people whose spiritual energy ought to be directed elsewhere.

The Elect on what should matter to concerned black people, exhibit A: "Unequal outcomes mean unequal opportunity."

Perhaps the star message received by whites "doing the work" of mastering Elect ideology in 2020 was that if black people lag behind whites in some way, the only reason must be racism, even if it's hard to perceive its role.

Since the 1960s, that idea has been central in debates over race, and it is much of why they are considered "complex." With racism no longer as overt as it was in the old days, it is considered a mark of sophistication to understand that the black guy having problems in 2020 is shackled by racism just as his great-grandfather was under Jim Crow, or his great-great-great-great-grandfather was under slavery. The nut of the issue has always been that if we don't trace the problems to racism, then the only other possibility must be that black people are inherently deficient somehow. Given how vastly unlikely that seems, we must point to racism.

That, for example, is a fair summation of the philosophy of Ibram Kendi. When the Elect hold up his work as essential, the thumbnail-sketch reason is this point of his, which parallels Ta-Nehisi Coates's famously eloquent tweet that "There's nothing wrong with black people that the complete and total elimination of white supremacy would not fix." Anyone reading this book must internalize this basic idea as a principal sticking point in why race debates get so fruitlessly heated. The implication is that if you don't think racism was the culprit, then you are a racist.

Indicative of the sea change is that in 2020 in Washington State, a conference of science teachers were treated to this assertion, emblazoned in PowerPoint: "If you conclude that outcome differences by demographic subgroup are a result of anything other than a broken system, that is, by definition, bigotry."

Throughout Kendi's prose runs a sense that he is doing us a favor in stating this very point without raising his voice, metaphorically turning his palms out with a quiet shrug as if to say, "What else can I tell you, and why should I have to ask?" This, folks, is why you are supposed to not just respect but worship him—as in treat his "ideas" as beyond criticism.

But the reason we ask him whether all racial disparities result from bigotry—if we have the guts to—is because the assertion is an oversimplification (as almost all of us know good and well). Much of the reason we warily refer to race discussions as "the race thing" is because anybody knows, if only deep down, that "racism" does not explain everything that ails the black community—and not even "systemic" racism. Much discussion of "the race thing" is a compact that educated Americans make to perform exchanges that step around logic in favor of placation and virtue signaling.

To the reader who feels like I am reaching them but feels conflicted about saying it out loud, let's look at real life.

In 1987, a rich donor in Philadelphia "adopted" 112 black sixth graders, few of whom had grown up with fathers in their home. He guaranteed them a fully funded education through college as long as they did not do drugs, have children before getting married, or commit crimes. He also gave them tutors, workshops, and after-school programs, kept them busy in summer programs, and provided them with counselors for when they had any kind of problem.

Forty-five of the kids never made it through high school. Of the sixty-seven boys, nineteen became felons. Twelve years later, the forty-five girls had had sixty-three children between them, and more than half had become mothers before the age of eighteen.

So what exactly was the "racism" that held these poor kids back that could have been erased at the time and created a different result for these children? The answer is none. Social history is too complex to yield to the either/or gestures of KenDiAngelonian propositions. What held those poor kids back was that they had been raised amid a different sense of what is normal than white kids in the burbs.

That is, yes, another way of saying "culture," and the sky will not fall in if we say so. Those cultural factors can certainly be traced to racism in the past, such as dehumanization leading a people to see themselves as separate from the norms of their surrounding society. Or, less comfortable to point out: in the late sixties white leftists encouraged poor black women to sign up for welfare payments they hadn't previously thought they needed, the leftists hoping that this would cause the collapse of the economy and force a restart. In the wake of this, subsequent generations of poor black people came to think of it as a normal choice to not work for a living. Not that this was the choice most people made in poor black communities—but only after this hard-leftist drive to make as many black people sign up for welfare as possible did it become one of many norms in poor black communities to not work nine to five, whether you were a man or a woman. Even poor black people before about 1966 would have seen the norm afterward as bizarre.

Whew! Yes, I know that sounds like I am making it up, but it is simple fact, and I must refer you to sources like my *Winning the Race* for presentation of the details. I can tell you in full confidence that so very much of what perplexes many readers here traces to what these supremely effective leftists accomplished via the National Welfare Rights Organization in the late 1960s—do look up the NWRO.

But it means that *through no fault of their own*, it was not resources, but those unconsciously internalized norms in the wake of what *whites taught them to embrace*, that kept those kids from being able to take advantage of what they were being offered. That same problem runs throughout endless ethnographies of inner-city folk up to right now, such as Katherine Newman's *No Shame in My Game*, Jason DeParle's *American Dream*, and Alice Goffman's *On the Run*.

———

The Philly story was not a fluke. Kansas City, same era: Twelve new schools were built to replace crummy ones black students had been mired in for decades. The effort cost $1.4 billion. The new schools included broadcast studios, planetariums, big swimming pools, and fencing lessons. Per-pupil spending was doubled, while class size was halved to about twenty-five students per class. Elementary school students all got their own computers, and there were now fifty-three counselors for them where before there had been none.

Fade out, fade in: Dropout rates stayed the same, the achievement gap between white and black students sat frozen, and the schools ended up needing security guards to combat theft and violence. The reason for this was nothing pathological about the kids, but it wasn't a "racism" that anyone could simply "eliminate," either. The racism in question had been threaded subtly through the endless currents and eddies of decades of social history leading to that moment.

The story of how black inner cities got to the state they were in by the 1980s is complex and has nothing to do with blame. However, to simply frame the issue as a "racism" that requires "elimination" now simply solves no problems. For example, one might say that one cause of the problems was that the war on drugs sent so many men to prison and left boys growing up in poverty, without fathers. But to call the war on drugs racist ignores that the laws it has been based on had hearty support from serious black people, including legislators as well as people living in poor communities. This time read *Black Silent Majority*, by Michael Fortner (who is black). Are we really going to say that those black people were too dumb to see the "racism" in the laws they supported as helping make them safer in their daily lives?

The failure of so many thinkers to understand the difference between the effects of racism in the past and racism in the present has strangled discussions about race for decades. The issue is so urgent to understand that we must visit one more example.

Black students tend to lag behind others in scholarly performance.

Many have argued that this is because of an idea among black teens that to embrace school is "acting white."

Much of the black punditocracy cringes to see white people reading anyone who calls attention to this, worried that the "acting white" argument could be taken as implying that there is something wrong with black kids just in themselves, rather than with society and its racism. But they miss that deficiency and racism are not the two sole possible explanations for the discrepancy.

In *Acting White: The Ironic Legacy of Desegregation*, a book as key to understanding race in America as Michelle Alexander's *The New Jim Crow*, Stuart Buck points out that many black students placed in previously all-white schools in the 1960s encountered widespread hostility, both overt and covert. White teachers thought of them as hopeless prospects for success, at best, and actively sabotaged their studies, at worst. Many of the white students, while not as belligerent toward them as the sneering kids in photographs of Little Rock Central High School, were distinctly unwelcoming to the new black kids in countless ways.

This will surprise few of us today, and it was hardly limited to the South: Recall the famous shot of the angry white woman at the meeting on busing in Boston. The pique she displayed did not magically evaporate once black kids were settled into these white schools. It became the substrate of the black kids' new schoolroom experience, week in and week out. That kind of rejection can make a person disidentify from a whole environment, and one result was a sense that school was for white kids, something outside of the authentic black experience.

This, to be sure, was because of racism. But over time, open white resistance to black kids in these schools receded as attitudes on race changed. Nonetheless, a cultural meme casting school as "white" had set in, and it has become self-perpetuating since.

Here is where the Kendi type of analysis—that black kids' problem with grades today is because of a "racism" that we need to simply "eliminate"—stubs a toe. I sense that people like him genuinely suppose that all cultural traits constitute direct responses to current conditions, such as that a diet heavy in fats and sugar must be caused by the difficulty in obtaining fresh vegetables in the neighborhood.

But in reality, cultural traits often persist beyond their original stimulus, having become subconsciously transmitted habit. The "acting white" charge is one of these cultural traits that has lasted beyond what created it. Black students may level the charge even in extravagantly funded schools where non-white teachers are as exquisitely sensitized about racism as humans can be, quite unlike the nasty, dismissive teachers that black kids encountered decades ago. This has been conclusively documented in rigorous ethnographic studies such as anthropologist John Ogbu's *Black American Students in an Affluent Suburb*.

It truly confounds a great many to imagine that a meme would persist beyond what caused it. They are perplexed (and annoyed) at the proposition that this "acting white" charge could live on if racism weren't the stimulus. Let's try this sequence of propositions:

A. Human behavior can be more habit-bound than pragmatic. For example, blood feuds among Albanians began because of concrete causes, but over time they persisted as simply what new generations felt as "what we do, what we are."

B. Black people are humans.

C. Black people can harbor habit-bound rather than pragmatic traits as well.

Perhaps the term *legacy*, usually familiar and comfortable to them, is useful? The Tuskegee experiment, leaving black men untreated for syphilis, understandably has left many wary of hospitals up until the present day, despite that the medical system, though still flawed, would never subject people to such barbarity now. The "acting white" meme has survived for exactly the same kind of reason.

It won't work to say that black Americans are for some reason immune to counterproductive memes in a way that no other humans ever have been. Why exactly would a tragic history render a people immune to ever developing problematic cultural traits? We in fact know that slavery and Jim Crow do not explain the "acting white" trope, because, as Stuart Buck outlined, black Americans a step past slavery were overtly famished for schooling, to a degree that seems almost odd, given the wariness of it that would hobble their distant descendants.

Social history is complicated. It's why people spend eons in training in it, and doing it well requires more than simply identifying how whites have been racists and leaving it there. The real social historian gets, for example, that a meme can be especially tenacious when it happens to be useful for other purposes. Teens of all stripes seek ways of defining their subgroup, fostering a sense of group membership, and even acting out. In black teen culture, one way of doing this is to embrace the idea that studying is white, passed on from previous peer cohorts even if the openly racist teachers of the 1960s and early '70s are now long gone. Even if you never knew those teachers, the idea that hitting the books isn't "us" feels good regardless, because you are a human being with naturally tribalist impulses.

Yes, white kids get made fun of for being nerds, too. But, as law professor Kimberly Norwood (who is black) has noted in her study of the "acting white" charge, it's one thing to be called a nerd, but another to be told you are disqualifying yourself from your race. That lends a particular sting.

Let's pull the camera back. Is the reason black kids often think of school as white that white people today don't like them, or that the system is somehow set against black kids learning?

No: That analysis makes no sense, period. Only a heedless, numb kind of fealty, a quiet refusal to engage the actual individuals we are talking about, would insist that "racism" is why a black kid, decades after 1966, gives a black nerd trouble for studying hard. Racism sparked this problem originally, to be sure, but the solution today cannot be to wave a magic wand and "eliminate racism," because the teachers who exerted racism upon black kids three generations ago are now mostly dead.

But the Elect analysis must see racism, and thus comes Ibram Kendi's "idea" that our whole metric for evaluating scholarly success must be overturned in favor of pretending that black kids should be measured as smart on the basis of "desire to know." For all of the warmth that notion may seem to have in being labeled as antiracism, it leaves black kids nowhere. That vision of antiracism means no George Washington Carver, whose miracles with the peanut were not driven by idle curiosity or some kind of alternate science of the streets. He worked within the Euro-American paradigm. The snazzy-looking little View-Master of our postwar memories was designed by a black man, Charles Harrison. He used the same skills as white designers of his time. Savory black spontaneity, in-touch-ness, and what Kendi airily describes as "desire to know" would have done nothing to help him.

To be Elect is to insist that unequal outcomes mean unequal opportunity, which is false. The misimpression misdirects our efforts at change, by inculcating in us a blindness to how a society actually operates. The insistence on this mantra makes us dumb.

The Elect on what should matter to concerned black people, exhibit B: "Slavery is hushed up."

Imagine this: A traveling museum exhibit of artifacts from the *Henrietta Marie* slave ship breaks attendance records in twenty cities. The magazine *Scientific American* has a page with excerpts from past issues, most of them, naturally, about science, but in one issue is featured a quotation from March 1851: "The population of the United States amounts to 20,067,720 free persons, and 2,077,034 slaves." The magazine gives it the headline "Open Sore." A white Washington State representative agitates to have Jefferson Davis's name removed from a Seattle highway and replaced with the name of a black Civil War veteran. In Cincinnati, Underground Railroad buffs—white ones—decry historical errors and distortions in a planned National Underground Railroad Freedom Center.

So much changed in 2020, right? Except these things happened in 2001 and 2002.

Yet we are to insist that America is in a perpetual "denial" about slavery, despite that one could compile collections of events like the above from every year since 2002, and backward about twenty from then. The success of the book *Roots* and then the smashing impact of the television miniseries in 1976; widely discussed films such as *Amistad* and *12 Years a Slave* and *Django Unchained*; weighty tomes earnestly covered in the media, such as Hugh Thomas's *The Slave Trade*; the New-York Historical

Society's marvelous exhibit about slavery in New York in 2005—one could continue endlessly.

Ta-Nehisi Coates urges "the end of scarfing hot dogs on the Fourth of July while denying the facts of our heritage." But this is the divorcé who can't stand seeing his ex have a good time. To tar today's America as insufficiently aware of slavery is more about smugness and noble victimhood than forging something new and needed.

To wit: Is there any degree of saturation to which slavery could reach into the American consciousness that would satisfy the Elect, such that they would allow that a battle had been won?

To hope that every American—white everyman in South Dakota, Indian American Silicon Valley entrepreneur, Korean immigrant grandma, American-born Latina hospice care supervisor, daughter of Bosnian immigrants pursuing her social work degree, Republican councilwoman in Texas, Cherokee police chief—will be wincing thinking about plantations while biting into their Independence Day weenie, even in a metaphorical sense, is utterly pointless. Pointless in that it will never happen, and pointless in that it doesn't need to.

I can guarantee that, psychologically, black America does not need its fellow countrymen to be quite that sensitized. A poll would reveal it instantly, as would just asking some black people other than the Elect ones, and the reader likely readily senses that. I can also guarantee that profound social change can happen without the entire populace being junior scholars about racist injustice. Such change has been happening worldwide for several centuries.

But Elect ideology requires you to classify what I just wrote as blasphemy and claim endlessly that slavery is a big secret in America. Year after year, Elect people announce that George Washington or Thomas Jefferson owned slaves, with the implication that this is hot news "no one wants to talk about," in media sources that have eagerly invited their wisdom and that of like-minded people for eons now. Notice: *These people will never admit that the Founding Fathers' slaveholding is no longer a secret.* The point is too central to their religious faith to allow concession.

To be Elect is to insist that America hushes up slavery. This is a falsehood. It endlessly distracts minds that would be better put to work addressing real problems.

The Elect on what should matter to concerned black people, exhibit C: "Historical figures who weren't woke on race must be canceled."

The Elect think that if a historical figure had slaves (Washington) or was ensconced in the slave trade (John Locke), or even was not hotly interested in dismantling slavery when they could have played a part in it—Alexander Hamilton has come under fire for that—then this must be the main thing we remember them for. They should be recalled only with condemnation.

They are useful to us only as object lessons in how not to be. Their achievements otherwise should be treated as footnotes, largely of interest only to the historian. Their backwardness on race must cling to them in our minds the way a gendered definite article must cleave in our minds to a French noun. *La plume*; George Washington, *le* slave owner.

This is obtuse, quite frankly. I won't write "dumb," because this would imply that people who make this kind of argument lack the insight to understand its hollowness. Deep down, almost all of them simply must.

It is very hard to see beyond what is normal in your time. Someone who grew up seeing black people as almost nothing but unpaid servants could not help but process this as normal, was vanishingly unlikely to argue against it, and—yes—likely ended up thinking of black people as inherently inferior. The Elect teach us to willfully fashion a numbness to basic logic on this issue, for the purposes of rhetoric and passion. That is, their argument here is cognitively sequestered: *religious.*

Thus, we are not to celebrate that America got past accepting slavery, but to reach backward in time and slap at the people who had yet to, in order to show how goodly we are now. The Elect require that we pretend that figures of the past are walking around with us, as if time does not pass. At best, this is the higher reasoning of quantum physics on the space-time continuum. But at worst, it is willful dummity. (Yes, I intend the word, which I made up. It summons how profoundly goofy this way of processing history is.)

We certainly don't need statues of people whose *main con-*

tribution to history was to enshrine slavery. Goodbye to public monuments to Robert E. Lee. And there are gray zones. Woodrow Wilson was more racist than the typical person of his time, place, and educational level, which makes many comfortable with seeing his name removed from buildings. It may surprise some that I am one of them. However, some think we should cherish Wilson's general record as a progressive with a passionate commitment to world peace, and I cannot say that they are wrong. The Elect, however, simply shudder that Wilson was a racist and can see nothing but heresy in any talk about him, his life, and his legacy other than that, as if Wilson had been retweeting white nationalists on his phone last week.

But defacing statues of George Washington? Sure, we can know that people like him had a blot on their records by our standards. But for the knowing to require that their bigotry be the main reason we engage them today, with any straying for too long beyond their racism processed as—(think about it) impious!—is a needless, thoughtless proposition.

In the future, the bulk of Americans may consider being pro-choice immoral. The celebration of any conglomeration of cells chemically set to become a *Homo sapiens* as "a person" may spread to intellectuals of influence and become as intelligentsia-chic as Electness is now. How do we feel about people of 2100 advocating that educators not celebrate the achievements of people in 2020 because they were not opposed to abortion?

Or why are today's Elect not roasting Barack Obama for his having espoused gay marriage only after he "evolved" to it? Note that we are to pretend not to understand history and circumstance only when the figures are white. Who even believes that the kid from Hawaii who smoked a lot of weed and also did "some blow," traveling in Ivy League circles in the 1980s and beyond, ever had any real problem with gay people getting married? Obama and I are close in age, and I lived in New York in the mid-eighties. Roll the dice again and I could have gotten high with him somewhere on the Upper West Side when we were both twenty-somethings, and I can all but guarantee you that the person who he was would not have had a problem with gay people getting married.

When Obama told voters that he did, he was dissimulating as a thoroughly sensible political feint, and the Elect pardon Obama for it, allowing an "evolution" of a kind that could never rehabilitate other figures in their minds—for example, Washington after freeing his slaves. Apparently Obama's (supposed) homophobia was okay because he is "intersectional"—as in, because his brown skin placed him under the thumb of white hegemony, it's okay that he was homopho . . . But see? There is no logic here.

A "meme" might be: Imagine a black boy of the inner city who sees a statue of Abraham Lincoln. He has been taught that Lincoln for a while thought black people, after emancipation, should be relocated to Africa and also did not see black people as whites' equals. The boy has a spasm of fury at the dismissal of his people and his self emanating from the statue, and splashes it furiously with paint. This is a vignette that could come straight out of an alternate-universe version of Randall Robinson's reparations book *The Debt*.

However stirring we find that scenario, however symbolic of the psychological effects of a tragic ancestral history, almost none of us see that boy as acting from logic or reason. Almost all of us know that, all in all, Lincoln deserves celebration for the totality of his legacy, despite his imperfections. We see the boy as—even if understandably—losing his head. We feel sorry for him. We pity him. But we want to hold him off, calm him down. Lincoln emancipated the slaves, an action that no president before him would have even considered, and that several after him likely wouldn't have, either, if slavery had persisted. (Grover Cleveland's Emancipation Proclamation?) We do not give the boy a book contract.

All grown-ups here in the real world ready to tar practically anyone living before about ten minutes ago as moral perverts because they were racists by our standards deserve the same judgment as does that boy, and as would a white boy who jumps the statue out of a furious identification with black people.

To be Elect is to insist that figures in the past might as well be living now, and that they thus merit the judgments we level upon present-day people, who inhabit a context unknown to those who lived before. As many kids would spontaneously understand, this is false. As to whether adults know something they don't, I suggest trying to explain to a fifth grader the case for yanking down the Lincoln Memorial.

To the extent that no one would look forward to having to kabuki their way through that, we know that this witch-hunting against long-dead persons is a distraction from doing real things for people who need help here in the present.

Do you really want to own this religion?

Do understand: You cannot live gracefully as an Elect while carefully disavowing the above. This is not a buffet; the Elect is a prix fixe affair. Try being selective in order to retain rationality while ducking an online roasting as a white supremacist and you will be quickly frustrated in the effort. If you want the grits, you have to take the gravy. You are in Russia under Stalin. You no more question KenDiAngelonian gospel than you question Romans or Corinthians. The Elect are not about diverseness of thought. Eliminating it, on race issues, is their reason for being.

Are you ready to be savaged for championing common sense, reason, and treating people as genuine equals, while being told that doing so is inappropriate when black people are involved, and that this is called "antiracism"?

The Elect's harm to black people is so multifarious and rampant that anyone committed to this religion and calling it antiracist walks in a certain shame.

5

BEYOND "DISMANTLING STRUCTURES": SAVING BLACK AMERICA FOR REAL

I F YOU HAVE READ me sniping for four chapters at what the Elect think we need to do, you may justifiably want to know what I would prefer as an alternative.

In this quick chapter, I shall tell you, and then in my final chapter I will explain how we can work toward something like it despite the Elect among us pursuing their charismatic but self-directed, sociopolitically futile, and quietly racist alternative.

The idea that what Americans need to do is simply "get rid of racism" is a ten-year-old's version of political progress. Racism refers not just to prejudice but also to societal inequity; racism is also a matter of past as well as present attitudes and policies. Something this protean, layered, and timeless must be ever restrained as much as possible, but it is impossible to simply get rid of. More to the point, doing so is not necessary.

What ails black America in the twenty-first century would

yield considerably to exactly three real-world efforts that combine political feasibility with effectiveness: There should be no war on drugs; society should get behind teaching everybody to read the right way; and we should make solid vocational training as easy to obtain as a college education.

Plank 1: End the war on drugs.

First, there should be no war on drugs. Even more potent drugs such as heroin should be available, albeit regulated, to those who seek them. Because drugs like these are illegal, there is a thriving black market for them. Underserved black men often drift into this black market, as an understandable choice when schools have failed them, and they know little about how to forge a life in the world beyond the one they have known—a world in which they have no personal connections.

Selling drugs makes few rich, but it becomes a way of getting by, while working with people you know, who are from the world you are comfortable in. I am quite sure that if I had grown up the way men like this do, I would choose selling drugs on the corner over trying to get through something called college and seeking a job wearing a suit among white people I thought of as distant, suspicious aliens.

But I am also quite sure of this because I believe in the strength of black people: If there were no such black market for hard drugs, the same men would get legal jobs.

Any legal work would be better than selling drugs, which

puts people at high risk of being killed or at least going to prison for long stretches and becoming even less employable, as well as often leaving children behind to grow up without a father. Only some of the federal and state prison populations are there as a direct result of drug sales, but vast numbers of them are in prison for murders or theft that are themselves connected to drug sales, such as through turf wars between gangs that thrive on drug sales.

The war on drugs, meanwhile, is universally agreed not to have worked in any case. Its eclipse would create a black American community in which even men dealt a bad hand would likely work legally, spells in prison would be rare, and thus growing up fatherless would be occasional rather than the norm. Antiracism should focus strongly on ending the war on drugs, and there is no need for legions of whites to be instructed in how privileged they are for this to happen.

Plank 2: Teach reading properly.

There are two ways to teach a child to read. Phonics is one, where you teach kids to sound out letters, and highlight the awkwardly spelled words separately. The other method is called the whole word method, which teaches kids to approach words as chunks, guessing at how they are pronounced based on their initial letter and context, the idea being that English spelling is too irregular for it to be worth it to teach kids to sound out letters.

Since the 1960s, phonics has been unanimously demonstrated to be more effective at teaching poor kids to read. Middle-class kids from book-lined homes often manage to guess their way into learning how to read via something like the whole word method. A "light just goes on," as parents of such kids describe it. However, that light does not often turn on for kids from homes without many books, where language is mostly oral. Kids like this need to be, well, taught to read.

Yet there are school districts throughout the United States where kids are taught to read either via the whole word method or via a hybrid one, when, again, studies show that just phonics is what works. Again and again, school districts that switch to phonics raise the test scores of black kids vastly, but the word never gets out on a national level. How teachers are instructed to teach reading (if they are at all) operates independently of the actual science of reading. I recommend Richard Seidenberg's *Language at the Speed of Sight* for the details.

This may seem an inside-baseball issue, but it is essential to getting past race in America. Generations of black kids, disproportionately poor, have been sideswiped by inadequate reading instruction. To find reading a chore puts a block on learning math, or anything else, from the page and is a perfect pathway to finding "the school thing" tiresome and irrelevant. The impact on life trajectory is clear.

I suspect many middle-class people have not had the experience of watching a nine- or ten-year-old kid, cognitively normal, looking at a page or a sign and reading it out with the diligent but labored air we associate more with someone two or three years younger, moving their lips and talking of "what it says," having yet to make the leap to fully silent reading, where the words are instantly processed bits of meaning. I suspect even fewer have had the experience of seeing cognitively normal people of twenty-five and older reading in this way, hobbled by poor reading training during childhoods in which few around them were recreational readers who could make up for the pedagogical deficit via cultural modeling.

This shouldn't be the norm, and antiracism should be centered in part on making school boards across America embrace phonics, or, in industry parlance, direct instruction.

Plank 3: Get past the idea that everybody must go to college.

We must revise the notion that attending a four-year college is the mark of being a legitimate American, and return to truly valuing working-class jobs. Attending four years of college is a tough, expensive, and even unappealing proposition for many poor people (as well as middle-class and rich ones). Yet the left endlessly baits applause with calls for college to be made more widely available and less expensive, with the idea that anyone who does not get a four-year college degree has been mired without "opportunity."

Yet people can, with up to two years' training at a vocational institution, make a solid living as electricians, plumbers, hospital technicians, cable television installers, body shop mechanics, and many other jobs. Across America, we must instill a sense that vocational school—not "college" in the traditional sense—is a valued option for people who want to get beyond what they grew up in.

The next time you employ a mechanic, plumber, cable installer, or ultrasound technician, ask yourself if that person seems to conceive of themselves as having been denied opportunity. Are they living a hardscrabble existence as they casually mention leading ordinary lives with their spouses and children—the latter of whom they often are putting through college?

That's it?

Two likely objections:

1: WHY SO FEW PLANKS?

Some will find this list a little short. Racism is a big problem. Black America has a lot of problems. Wouldn't a legitimate platform include a good ten or eleven planks?

No, actually. Part of what makes a platform pragmatic is processability.

An array of ten-plus distinct ideas is more a display than a plan for action—as in what we can actually imagine getting through Congress or adopted by a critical mass among fifty states. It may seem commensurate with the scope of the tragedy to present a flotilla of reform ideas, complete with busy-looking graphics, as if in doing that we acknowledge grievance and legacy with an appropriate gravity.

But in terms of how real life works in a vast, highly diverse, and politically polarized nation, to insist that black America can change only via a redux of the awesome, throw-paint-at-the-wall array of the Great Society efforts is a kind of utopianism, and utopianism is its own reward.

To propose a vast slate of demands, each carefully bullet-pointed into four or five sub-demands, is a battle pose that intrigues for a bright, shining moment, only for implacable reality to overtake it in short order. Can we dream? Sure—but of things that can actually happen. Utopianism lacks sophistication. It is the game of performers, not those who actually get things done for real people.

My pragmatism stems not from some kind of baked-in "conservatism" but from the lessons of history. A great many concerned people have proposed Marshall Plan–style slates of proposals for the black American community, and their fate is ever Ozymandian.

In the 2010s, Black Lives Matter composed one of these long lists of demands, which has had no impact on black lives since.

Commentator Tavis Smiley took a similar approach in various books, forums, and speeches in the 1990s and 2000s, and despite his sincerity and commitment, these "demands" never gained any purchase among people in power, and thus changed no black communities.

Going further back, the Great Society effort was the one time when circumstance allowed America to actually put into action a vast raft of programs directly targeting poor black communities. It is universally agreed that even these had very little lasting effect. As to those who say not enough was done, in my experience they cannot tell you just what or how much more would have had an effect and why. Frankly, they are often also not aware of just how very much actually was offered and funded for black communities in the era. It was a long time ago.

We need a more precisely targeted approach to black America's problems, focusing on changes that (1) have an actual chance of making it into legislation and budgeting, (2) come with further gains built in—for example, ending the war on drugs will make vocational training more attractive to more poor young black men who will then help get the word out—and (3) are of a compact number, forming a single, coherent, and memory-friendly effort rather than a diffuse alphabet soup.

2: WHAT ABOUT THE POLICE?

Notably absent from my list of reforms is the police.

I heartily espouse police reform but consider it unlikely that anything can be done to stop cops from firing their weapons lethally in tight or even risky situations. I know this partly because, even in the wake of George Floyd's murder, throughout 2020 cops continued killing or maiming people, despite all eyes upon them, with no real consequences. Jacob Blake and Daniel Prude were the black ones most covered, with the general assumption that cops do this only to black people. The sad underground truth is that they do it to all kinds of people all the time, but this is not the place to dwell on that talking point. The key is that changing the cops will take eons; changing black lives should take less time than that.

However, with no war on drugs, encounters between black men and the cops will be rarer. No cops will be sent to poor neighborhoods to sniff out people selling or carrying drugs or to break up drug-selling rings, nor will cops be assigned to sit roadside waiting to stop people for drug possession. Furthermore, better-educated people with solid jobs, raised more often by two parents able to focus their full attention upon them, will be that much less likely to end up in ugly encounters with the police.

ELECT IDEOLOGY IS PRESENTED with great charisma. In our current climate, it can be mighty difficult to perceive that this seeming wisdom is actually poisonous. However, we must keep front and center that Elect philosophy is two things: performative and racist.

On the performativity, the Elect claim to be committed to making lives better for people. Yet quite often, their positions run orthogonally to forging change in the real world. Think of how seldom you see Elect wisdom presented in actual and sustained connection to change happening on the ground. In fact, to focus on actual processes of making change is derided by core

Elect philosophy as "solutionism" (many will recall the term from *White Fragility*), a hasty attempt to get past the discomfort of self-examination.

The real job to these people is supposed to be tarring others for heretical thoughts, talking only vaguely about how that is necessary in order to "dismantle structures." Whites must be held at metaphorical gunpoint and demanded to do "the work" of becoming "antiracist" in their every waking moment and to despise themselves for lapses in doing so, despite that it is a work they are condemned never to finish. This is performance art.

On racism, Elect philosophy teaches black people that cries of weakness are a form of strength. It teaches us that in the richness of this thing called life, the most interesting thing about you is that the ruling class doesn't like you enough. It teaches us that to insist that black people can achieve under less than perfect conditions is ignorant slander. It teaches us that we are the first people in the history of the species for whom it is a form of heroism to embrace the slogan "Yes, we can't!" Elect philosophy is, in all innocence, a form of racism in itself. Black America has met nothing so disempowering—including the cops—since Jim Crow.

But goodness, the Elect make a good pitch regardless, partly because they truly believe what they are saying. "Dismantling structures," "social justice," "decentering whiteness"—if I were white and wanted to do the right thing on race, I would be confused.

"The black writers everybody tells me are the right ones say I'm supposed to think being black gives you a pass on criticism, and that I'm supposed to make way for whatever they ask for, plus also hate myself."

"Then there are these controversial ones who say to stop treating them like children. I know they aren't crazy, but neither are the ones in the *Times* and on MSNBC, and some of them practically weep on the air, they are so sincere about these things. What do I do?"

"That young Coleman Hughes is *so* smart, but come on, Ta-Nehisi Coates is such a brilliant writer. I learned some things watching Glenn Loury—come on, he isn't crazy—but Ibram Kendi wears dreadlocks!" (So sorry—I just had to.)

I suggest a handy kit. However you possibly can, you should:

1. Fight to end the war on drugs.

2. Make sure kids not from book-lined homes are taught to read with phonics.

3. Advocate vocational training for poor people and battle the idea that "real" people go to college.

But one must do whatever one has chosen from the above while also resisting the Elect. That can be difficult, and I offer counsel in the final chapter.

6

HOW DO WE WORK
AROUND THEM?

T HERE ARE TWO WAYS of understanding the title of this
chapter. We need to know how to work our way around
the Elect, and also how to get real work done with the Elect
around us, which they will always be. As such, I will propose
first what not to do, and then what to actually do.

The issue, more specifically, is how to constructively manage an ideological reign of terror. The depth of Americans' terror at being tarred as racists stands as one of many contradictions
to the pessimistic attitude of the Elect toward America's progress on the race question. Most Americans' racial attitudes have
progressed massively beyond what they were a few decades ago.
However, today Americans mainly experience this enlightenment as something they fear being told they lack, by people who
consider it their duty to refuse to listen to you, whose pro-
grammed response to any departure from their creed is verbal
nunchucks.

Life is short; we pick our battles. The scoffing, the facial expressions, the sarcastic *ummm*s and eye rolls and clever GIFs—this stuff is *menacing* unless you are the unusual kind of person who enjoys arguing with people and doesn't mind being hated. If any of these people happen to single you out and get in your face, you might be inclined to just cave and nod—give them anything they want just so they move on and go away. The Elect, in terms of the combined effects of their warriors and their quiet supporters, are today a mob, pure and simple. They are unreachable for the simple reason that they are arguing from religion rather than reason, trying to foist their dogma into the public square out of a misguided sense that they are the world's first humans to find the Answer to Everything.

The Elect must be othered. We must stop treating them as normal. Already, the term "woke" is used in derision, but using that term with a snicker is about as oppositional as many dare to be against this mob. It isn't enough. *How* do we step up with such a destructive current of cognitive interference in our way, wielded by people with power, and chilling us with the threat of social excommunication?

After insisting that what they are doing is about changing society rather than about virtue signaling, the Elect are especially given to claiming that the excesses and bizarreries and tragedies I have described are not a serious problem. People like me warning against the mobocracy of Electness are just obsessing over a few crazy overstretches and pretending it means the sky is falling in. But this argument does not go through. Let's go stepwise.

A. It's just some kids finding themselves.

But at Evergreen State, where just these sorts of kids hounded biology professor Bret Weinstein out of his job for refusing to vacate the campus on a day designated as a "safe space" day for minority students, many faculty members chimed in with this ideology. A quarter of them signed a petition asking for his disciplining. And as to individual professors, I will only direct you to check out, on the web, one Naima Lowe, whose insight about Weinstein and the administration who had been "harboring" him was (to lend a quick sample) "you can't see your way outta your own ass!"

Anyone with any familiarity with the Collegetown scene knows that the Elect are by no means only kids. Many of them are nearing retirement age and today enjoying a new sense of dominance. I first encountered the Elect—before they were becoming our national moral commanders—amid the debate over discontinuing racial preferences in the University of California system in 1995. Many of them even then were graying at the temples and then some. This is not about kids.

B. It's just something going on in some colleges and universities.

But Alison Roman worked for a newspaper. This is not 2015's issue, where the hot news was Charles Murray, while speaking at Middlebury, being not only shouted down but hounded off his platform by a crowd who jostled the car he and his assigned (left-leaning) interlocutor were in to such a degree that the interlocutor wound up in a neck brace. The ideology that drove that episode has jumped the rails in influence since, and especially in 2020, when this mindset was sanctioned as the sole one admissible as representing our nation's "reckoning" on race.

C. But Roman only got suspended (i.e., "Why'd he open his book with that?").
But she later left the paper. And Sue Schafer, the one who attended a party in blackface in mockery of a comment by Megyn Kelly, was simply fired from her job. As was Gary Garrels from the San Francisco Museum of Modern Art, as have been many others. In roughly 2015, that Roman would even have been suspended for what she said would have seemed about as likely as Donald Trump becoming president. Any who doubt that should consult a similar controversy over something Alessandra Stanley, employed by the same newspaper, said that offended some race-related sensibilities in 2014. She pushed back, and a lot of people continued to hate her, but she stayed in her post for the duration and the episode was forgotten. Today it is reasonable to suppose that she would have been canned.

D. This is just a philosophical tempest in a teapot among the Acela corridor elite. What really matters is real people suffering from day to day.

But if this is just about that bunch and their musings, then what about how Elect ideology is being presented as fundamental to child pedagogy in public and private schools nationwide? New York City's former schools chancellor Richard Carranza presented his teachers and staff with the idea that the written word, objectivity, being on time, and individuality are "white things." Yes, he was serving in a city on the Acela corridor, but the intent was to shape the minds of humble New York kids unlikely to ride the Acela anytime soon. Plus the same ideology is being foisted, as I write, on school districts all across the United States. This is a national issue, not one fetishized by a small bunch of northeasterners frustrated by the *New York Times* editorial page.

If you are reading this, you likely know that the stringent, anti-white, hyper-Elect tenets of *White Fragility* are being introduced into kiddie curricula nationwide. All of this is being done by worriedly smiling people sincerely under the impression that the national reckoning about race requires enshrining this Orwellian poppycock. The widespread treatment of that book as a biblical testament deep-sixes any claim that what I am writing about is merely something a few contrarians are getting their knickers in a twist about in a few northeastern metropolises. If the Elect are reaching our children, then this is real. Anyone who smirks "What's the big deal?" is either ignorant (possible), cynical (unlikely), too young to understand that the Overton window—that which we think of as normal—is shifting (understandable), or, quite simply, religious without knowing it.

E. The real problem is the right-wing, racist zealots who stormed the Capitol Building calling for the blood of Mike Pence and Nancy Pelosi.

This claim is a debate-team feint. As scary as those protesters were, which institutions are they taking over with their views? The question is not whether conservatism, in a much broader sense, dominates certain institutions and even societal structures. The question is: Which official institutions are bowing down to the militant physicality of *those who battled with police officers in the Capitol lobby?* Note that the answer is none.

"It could happen here." Okay, we must be wary, but in this case, where did "it" happen beyond one awful episode at the Capitol, which is vanishingly unlikely to ever happen again?

Meanwhile, no one can deny that Elect ideology has a stranglehold on institutions that barely knew it just a few years ago. The Elect are changing America, or at least what much of America is comfortable presenting itself as when threatened with slander. The Capitol mob are changing nothing. Seeing their awfulness from so close up felt like a change, but that was in us, not them. Novelty in our perception is a change within us as individuals; it is different from those we newly perceive actually penetrating institutions. That they tried to threaten democracy is less important than that their attempt failed. The Elect are resonant successes in comparison, despite that their sense of self-definition as *speaking truth to power* prevents them from acknowledging it directly.

What not to do.

So where do we go from here? First we need a list of what we don't need to do. I promise, it's short. Just three things we should always know.

1. THERE IS NO DISCUSSION TO BE HAD.

A person fully committed to Elect ideology is not amenable to constructive discussion. They will deny the charge, but what they mean by "discussion" is that we will learn their wisdom. Think of the convert to, say, Mormonism who recalls being swayed by "talking to" an elder. This is the kind of discussion the Elect may seek. However, they seek not conversation but conversion, which is why so many are so frustrated with the Elect. Attempts to break bread with them seem to do little but elicit their disgust with you.

It may feel natural to suppose that instead, it makes sense to ask the Elect to be more open to other views, to gently ask them to reconsider their dogmatism. Hence endless chin-scratching calls for them to understand the post-Enlightenment commitment to free speech and the like.

But to the Elect, this sounds like calling for pedophiles to be allowed their "diverse" point of view. Most of us would say pedophilia is particularly abhorrent in how perniciously it acts upon another person. To the Elect, power differentials and their results are the same kind of "harm," and we cannot understand what we are up against with these people without fully comprehending that. This is why they are often so smart and yet opposed to others having opinions different from theirs. The conflict here is, regrettably, not as simple as one that could be resolved by telling the Elect to just listen.

You don't ask a devout Christian why they can't "consider" reconceiving of Jesus as a man who simply passed away forever two thousand years ago, as all humans do, was never again sensate to human affairs of any kind, and thus did not and does not "love" them now. In the same way, you cannot "discuss" with an Elect whether they should prioritize logic and civility over their strain of antiracism. Their sense of priorities is fundamentally and unmovably different from those of someone unconverted to their worldview.

We must do an end run around these people, not make the mistake of thinking they are just "het up" or have wended a few yards into a wrong turn. The most charitable way of getting at what the Elect feel is that, from their point of view, to ask them to use sense or be nice on race issues is like asking a

Birmingham protester being fire-hosed to the ground to use sense and be nice. To the Elect, their intransigence *is*, in a long-term sense, a form of being nice, because they think of it as a prelude to a more moral society.

Ask whether microaggressions merit the same response as physical assault and the Elect do not receive this as a challenging query. To them, it is splitting hairs to taxonomize assault in this way. There is even some reality on their side, in that psychological stress and trauma have undeniable physiological consequences. The Elect ask: "Upon what grounds do we specify that a person harmed by policies, or even just words, must respond more decorously than someone harmed by fists and weapons?" Maybe it's an advance to classify all harms on the same level, such that in a future world, people are hurt by neither objects nor words or abstractions?

Or maybe not—but it is highly unlikely that an Elect interlocutor will be able to entertain the possibility of there being any question about such matters. We cannot penetrate this kind of reasoning any more than we could teach someone out of faith in Jesus, because this is a religion. We cannot reach it despite that it is what underlies the thinking of that person shouting down the room in a corporate "diversity" session, or that woke relative you can't get across to at Thanksgiving, or that editorial you read that sounds like it was written by someone in France in 1250 (or Selma in 1965) and yet is attracting thousands of likes per day by people praising it as channeling modern American reality.

As such, to ask, "Why are you decreeing that your opinion

is the only valid one?" is futile. The Elect don't see themselves as having "opinions." They are arguing from gospel, even though they don't call it that and are not consciously aware of it, which makes discussions with them even harder than ones about other religions. Perfectly understandable is how often their version of response is "Don't you disapprove of racism?" This is precisely where they are coming from—and only there. And only with *their* sense of what racism is.

At a certain point, a discussion about religion can end peacefully with "On this, we'll just have to disagree," with both sides understanding that at "faith," the two sides have nowhere left to go. In a discussion about racism, too often neither side understands that faith of the same kind is at issue. The Elect person thinks he or she is "simply correct," while the secular one actually supposes that they are engaged in an argument based on logic.

2. TO BE SENSIBLE ABOUT RACE IS NOT "BLAMING THE VICTIM."

For all of the attention that modern English speakers' usage of the word *like* as a hedging term attracts, all languages have a way of hedging in that way. The only question is what word or expression they use. In Mandarin, one hedges by saying "that, that, that . . . ," as if grasping for what the thing or concept is called. It happens that the expression for that in Mandarin is pronounced "nay-guh."

Here and there, black Americans have purported a certain

worry as to just what Chinese people are saying when they say "nay-guh," but this has always been a kind of joke. Yet it was only a matter of time before somebody decided it wasn't a joke anymore, and it is no accident that it finally happened in 2020.

Professor Greg Patton was teaching a class on business communication to students at the University of Southern California's Marshall School of Business and was discussing hedging terms in different languages. He in passing mentioned that in Mandarin people say "nay-guh, nay-guh, nay-guh." This offended a group of black students in the class, who reported Patton to the dean of the business school, claiming that "we were made to feel less than." The students claimed, "We are burdened to fight with our existence in society, in the workplace, and in America. We should not be made to fight for our sense of peace and mental well-being at Marshall."

Patton was, of course, suspended from teaching the class for the rest of the semester. But the problem is that these students were pretending. That sounds rash, but black students taking Chinese have been hearing "nay-guh" nationwide for decades without feeling discriminated against. A group of black residents in China even wrote to USC objecting that they had never experienced any injury from hearing the word. Worldwide, people observed that if these black USC students expected to be able to do business in China, they certainly couldn't expect Chinese people to censor themselves and not use the word around them. Overall, these students were extending their sense of

Elect linguistic prosecution to another language, which made no blessed sense whatsoever—to such an extent that they must have known.

To pretend they did not is to insult their intelligence, which they themselves sadly accomplished repeatedly in their complaint. They claimed that in spoken Chinese "nay-guh" is said with a pause between the two words, an absurdity. Do English speakers say not "you know" but "you . . . know"? And never mind that "nay-guh" is not a "synonym" of the N-word, as they stated, but a homophone (and even there, only somewhat). For the dean to give in to these students' demands that Patton be dismissed from the course was an insult to black people. A black student who feels that hearing a Mandarin hedge word that happens to sound kind of like the N-word deprives him of his "peace and mental well-being" urgently needs psychiatric counseling, a state of mind unlikely to apply to the number of students who decided to use Patton as the latest pawn in their drive to fashion their lives as passion plays of noble victimhood. These students were, in a word, acting.

This brings us to one of the knottiest points in this book, a grievously awkward fact: A lot of today's victimhood claims on race are fake. Ibram Kendi intones that being an antiracist means that we should engage solely with how the "victim" feels rather than with the "perpetrator's" explanations. But sometimes the explanations are valid, because the claim of victimhood is unwarranted. We are taught that a black person's claims of victimhood can never be unwarranted, on the basis of some overarching principle that cancels out reasoning. But to accept that is racist.

It implies that black Americans, and only we, are perfect. Whites who voted in a monster like Trump were mistaken; Albanians who carried blood feuds into the modern era were mistaken—but black Americans can never be wrong "because slavery and Jim Crow"? Or even "because slavery, Jim Crow, and Eric Garner"? This does not elevate black Americans; it demotes them. There is nothing about experiencing racism, as hideous as it is, that makes it cancel out what we otherwise assume as common sense about human nature.

The black Elect have a plan for that, the idea that impact, not intent, matters. But look past the weight of the words *impact* and *intent* and it leaves the question *intact* (!) as to just why black people can't ever misidentify racism as the reason for a problem. Why is it impossible that a black person may misinterpret something as racist, be given an explanation, and say, "Oh, okay—I beg your pardon," and walk away? "You have to respect how I feel," we are taught to unconditionally accept, with the implication that the "feeling" could logically arise only from racist mistreatment. But—get ready, this must be said, and, frankly, it's better said by someone black:

> As often as not today, what the person "feels" is based on what they have been taught to "feel" by a paradigm that teaches them to exaggerate and even fabricate the "feeling." In other words, much too often, the person who tells

you to accept and go from how they "feel" has been, as it were, coached.

This is just what the black Elect cringe to see a black writer say, and it will be hard for many readers to accept. The black person airing grievance is just acting? You are to listen to me saying that, when you have spent your life being drilled in the very opposite idea, that the black person's anger, no matter how disconsonant with an imperfect but seemingly negotiable reality, is rooted in a clear and present oppression rarely overt but ever droningly present "out there" in ways "hard to explain" but tragically real and insurmountable? Calling Dr. DiAngelo—haven't I transgressed here?

But come now. I have transgressed nothing but an arbitrary, punitive, and purposeless etiquette. Sure, sometimes the roots of grievance about racism are quite clear. No one will tell Eric Garner's family that they are being performative in their grief and indignation. But what about, well, so very often otherwise? A book the mainstream media pretends does not exist is Wilfred Reilly's *Hate Crime Hoax*, which calmly presents one case after another where black people in our era have been conclusively revealed to have fabricated scenarios where they were supposedly discriminated against or attacked for being black. One cannot come away from Reilly's book thinking this is a mere matter of the very occasional outlier chucklehead, and it flies in the face of smug calls to think only of impact rather than intent. And I must mention that Reilly is black.

For example, do you really believe that universities are racist institutions? In 2020, Princeton's Elects tarred their own institution as such, and Trump's Civil Rights Division threatened to investigate it for racism, forcing its leaders to actually outline how they have gone against what Civil Rights law specifies. Princeton got caught short by a noble but transparent lie, a massive signaling of virtue with no significant correspondence to fact. And remember, the Princeton Elects in question were not a bunch of kids acting up—this included a great many faculty and administrators with mortgages and gray hairs.

When cases like this come up, a part of you may want to just accept it on some level. Logic peeps its head up; you quietly press it back down, scoop some dirt over it, and pat the ground smooth, thinking of this as the modern person's version of intelligence and morality. But it never feels quite right, because it isn't. To allow claims from black people that no one would accept from their own children is racist. The idea that for black people it passes as authenticity to not make sense is racist.

The politesse of pretending that race issues don't have to make sense, that they are uniquely "deep," must go. It constitutes racist discrimination. If the designation of someone or something as racist seems incoherent, chances are it is just that: not "complex." Do not condescend to black people by pretending that nonsense, when it comes from us, is deep. If you truly see us as equals, you can—if only internally—call us on our bullshit. It's what you afford everyone else.

When a black person pretends they are hurt when a white

professor says Chinese people say "nay-guh" for "like," is speaking up for truth like telling someone being slapped it doesn't hurt? No. Go with your reason and admit it. It means calling even your favorite go-to sources on what qualifies as performance. *The New York Times* published an editorial in which an unfortunate black philosophy professor wrote:

> I almost never attend casual faculty functions. I don't go out for drinks. I don't entertain for dinner parties and I don't seek to ingratiate myself into the lives of my white colleagues. . . . It's already hard enough to breathe in America. Every day you feel like you're living with a knee on your neck.

What happened to George Floyd was revolting, and racism does exist. This professor was also once briefly but brusquely detained mistakenly by police officers. But if he has been left truly feeling afraid for his physical being in socializing with his white faculty colleagues in the year 2020 and feels like he lives with a knee on his neck daily, he is unwell. He should go on leave immediately and undergo psychoanalysis several days a week.

He is exaggerating out of a sense that it serves a larger purpose, and it does. He is an Elect black person who sees his value in the world not only as forging new views about Kant and Foucault and Fanon, as other philosophers do, but as calling attention to racism's role in American life and, in doing so, supposedly helping "dismantle structures." The *Times'* David Brooks quoted this piece in allegiance with the new mood, later announcing that he, as a conservative of sorts, had moved left on race. But in pretending that this person was writing about reality, Brooks was giving black thought a pass. This is not progressive thinking; it is unintended racism.

To classify any pushback against transparently ridiculous claims of injury as blaming the victim is to assume the victimhood as beyond question. This involves a senseless leap of logic that one only subscribes to in dread of being called out as something awful. Black Elect who exaggerate their victimhood are not doing so out of some kind of cynical quest for attention or power. They do it in a quest for a sense of significance that they miss from real life for various reasons, as I discussed in chapter 3. However, we infantilize them by pretending they are beyond question because "impact trumps intent."

The phrase "blaming the victim" must no longer be taken as a mic-drop no one can follow. The phrase has come to be used not as a teaching tool but as a battering ram.

3. LOGIC, NOT "AUTHENTICITY."

There is a place we must "go," a question that will hover over assessments of this book and which I see no reason to answer only in media interviews. The question is appropriately addressed right here and now: *Am I black enough to write this book?*

Namely, how much can you trust this book coming from me? A cardiganed college professor and writer, with his upbringing in leafy neighborhoods, educated in private schools, who has never had run-ins with police, writing and podcasting about his biracial children, and hard to see as truly "rooted" among black people less fortunate than he is. Is he, well, darn it, you know . . . *really* black?

Or, "Is he black *enough*?" Someone on the sidelines asks, "What does *that* mean?" and the answer might be, even if only thought rather than uttered, "He hasn't suffered. He doesn't know what it's really like for *real* bl—whoops, I mean, *most*—black people. He's speaking from the outside."

That question is not crazy. And its answer is this: The oppression of black people is supposed to be so cluelessly indiscriminate that all of us, regardless of class, background, demeanor, dress style, or accomplishment, are regularly subject to bigoted treatment. I suggest the *Times* op-ed by the philosophy professor as an example. The cops supposedly do not discriminate between me and the teenager, me and the "thug," me and anyone else with black American skin. That across-the-board contempt is supposed to be one of the prime motivators of anti-racism, after all—that *it's all about race*.

As such, it is incoherent to assume that because I am hopelessly bourgeois, I have been spared racism and therefore just don't understand. The only way out is to propose that I am just too naive to realize the endless racism I suffer. I reject that; it would mean I was a tad dim. Perhaps I'm clever enough but in denial? I doubt it—I know racism when I do encounter it, even when it's subtle, and have written about it often. And yet I still believe every word I am writing in this book.

Overall, there may remain a sense among some that views on race are closest to truth when coming from the hood. But the notion that only people who have been chased down the street by a cop can have opinions about race worth a listen is one of the saddest and most senseless versions of racial identity any human group has ever been saddled with.

I make no apologies for not being a character from *The Wire*. I am committed to getting help to black people who need it, and my positions in this book stand or fall on the basis of their applicability to that mission.

Back to basics.

So:

1. Elect philosophy is unreachable via discussion.

2. You are not "blaming the victim" if you reject Elect thought.

3. This book is not invalidated by the fact that its author grew up middle-class with two parents.

Where do we go now?

A white, highly educated friend of mine has been alive since 1980. She is quite aware of the ideological contours of our moment and its signature testaments. She is not the contrarian sort, but is independent enough a thinker to see some real problems with the new prosecutorial mood on the left. She happened to write me what I regard as a perfectly useful description of where a white American today can feel comfortable on whether they "get the race thing":

> I definitely don't worry that maybe I am a racist. I think lots of people think I should worry about that? That maybe all white people should be spending their time worrying about that these days? But there is nothing to worry about—I know that I don't harbor overtly prejudiced beliefs, and I know that I do have subconscious biases, but so does everybody else, and it's not a thing one can castigate oneself for. All you can do is do your best to let your rational mind overrule your subconscious when possible, and try to be aware of when it may not be working. The idea that my time and energy would be well spent feeling bad about the possibility that I won't do this perfectly seems ridiculous.

This is, of course, exactly what the Elect have decided is not enough. To them, my friend is a racist without knowing it, and the reason black America has problems is that people like her refuse to do the "work" of identifying the racist rot of their complicity in an unjust system. But folks, unless you are hate-reading this book, my friend is probably not unlike you. Black folks, you probably don't have any problem with her at all if you take her at her word in the statement.

Her views on race are light-years beyond the typical ones of people of her demographic as recently as 1980, and it's enough for all of us to work with. White Americans can go around with exactly the position my friend has and the political program I outlined in the previous chapter could still go forward. Tell me it would go forward faster or better if my friend felt worse about her "complicity," and I say show me how. Just what historical precedent is there where deep-seated guilt made ordinary members of the ruling class political junkies and changed the life conditions of poor people? Remember, anyway, that to the Elect, "solutionism," as in thinking about results, is a sin. What they are really up to is smoking out the sin—building the backyard fort, as it were.

The Elect are our Pharisees. In fostering antiracist ideas that actually harm black people, they are obsessed with the letter of the law rather than its spirit, and their prosecution of sinners contrasts with Jesus's embrace of them. We see in them not the demeanor of someone smoking out something awful— think of unearthing bodies after a mudslide—but the demeanor of someone rejoicing in *showing themselves to have* smoked out something awful. Their social media posts tend to be the equivalent of someone posting a picture not of the covered-up body they dug out of the mudslide, but of themselves actually in the act of digging the body out, to show that they were the ones who did it. This is the kind of "work" that the Elect are evangelizing America to do.

How about doing work motivated by something other than working out feelings of guilt and feeling superior to other people while enjoying a sense of belonging? The work we should do involves calling for the war on drugs to end, supporting phonics-based reading instruction, and celebrating every political move that helps dilute the conviction that all people need to spend four years living in a dorm before they start training for the workplace. That's work enough, and it will help change the world.

But there will remain the Elect reviling you for, or at least lecturing you about, this slimmed-down version of antiracism, and telling you that supporting it makes you a moral pervert. Here's what to do.

Just say no.

What we must do about the Elect is stand up to them. They rule by inflicting terror, either through invective or quietly trailing off with the likes of "Well, I guess if you think racism is okay, then . . ." They think that to require them to engage in actual reason is heretically "white." There is nowhere to go with them from there.

Our response to this cannot be to simply fold, because this means giving up the post-Enlightenment society we hold dear. We must stop being afraid of these people, and once we do, there is something we need to steel ourselves against and get used to.

People often ask, "How can I talk to people like this without being called a racist?"

The answer is: *You cannot.*

That is, they *will* call you a racist, no matter what you do or say beyond what they stipulate as proper. Black people: Be ready for the alternate slam, that you are "self-hating" and "betraying your own people." They *will* say this to and about you.

The coping strategy, therefore, must be not to try to avoid letting them call you a racist, but to *get used to their doing so and walk on despite it.*

Specifically, on top of all else we are required to manage, enlightened Americans must become accustomed to being called racists in the public square.

We must become more comfortable keeping our own counsel, and letting our own rationality decide whether we are racist, rather than entertaining the eccentric and self-serving renovated definitions of racism forced upon us by religionists.

When that type calls you a racist—and I mean white ones every bit as much as black ones—you need not walk off, "doing the work" of wondering whether your accuser was right. You are Galileo being told not to make sense because the Bible doesn't like it.

Does this seem a lot to ask? I ask no more than the Elect, who *demand* you suspend your disbelief and commit yourself to a worldview on social justice focused more on virtue signaling than helping people. If you are going to do "work," as we put it these days, wouldn't you rather do some that actually makes a difference beyond making innocent people cry?

Unless you choose to simply disengage, you are stuck with two alternate kinds of work to do. One kind requires that you pretend your rationality is invalid, to avoid someone trying to hurt your feelings. The other kind requires that you get used to a certain amount of acrid static in the air, while you follow your heart and mind and join those trying to make an actual difference for people who need it.

Yes, it will be easier for some to stand up to the Elect than others. Temperamentally, some are more comfortable with conflict than others. Some people's jobs require them to toe an Elect line more than others. Some people's incomes allow them to leave positions more easily than others. The decision must be individual.

However, even the general zeitgeist matters, and all can help to season that in ways large and small. We must do what we can within whatever perimeters life has placed around us, in just the way that the Elect teach us to ask what we can do within the boundaries of our lives to be "allies" in their version of social justice.

Wherever you are in a position to give an Elect the experience of calling you a dirty name and finding that you do not back down, you can contribute to a groundswell needed to put these people back in their place. Help set a new mood, even if only by refusing to heed the judgments of that little Elect angel on your shoulder when making decisions.

The idea is not to muzzle the Elect. We need the hard left to point us to new ways of thinking. However, we need them to go back to doing this while seated, with the rest of us, rather than standing up and getting their way by calling us moral perverts if we disagree with them and calling this speaking truth to power. We must disabuse them of the idea that the race discussion after George Floyd's death somehow revealed the morally incontestable necessity of America bowing down to the KenDiAngelonian religion.

Separation of church and state.

Standing up to this performance art will be easier if we always keep in mind that Elect philosophy is actual religion, pure and simple. We must exert the mental exercise of imagining them meeting in their own churches. University buildings now are all but indistinguishable from such churches. The Martian anthropologist would readily note that what we title educational institutions double as cathedral complexes for our intelligentsia's religious commitments. Widespread beliefs founded in transparently irrational assumptions, fiercely held by otherwise empirical people, for ulterior, transcendent reasons, are religion.

When we understand that the Elect are a religious body, we understand that their adherents have no business being the final arbiters on our school curricula or what is exhibited in a museum, on what subjects people choose to study or the conclusions they draw from them, or on what kind of morality is expected of our populace. As journalist Charles Fain Lehman has nicely put it, "To recognize something as a religion is to subject it to certain restraints; the strange new religions that seem so quickly to have spread merit no exception to this rule."

Also, the fact that many black people subscribe to this religion does not exempt it from this simple logic. "Precision is white." "Whites dating black people must be racist deep down." "Silence is violence." "Unequal outcomes mean unequal opportunity." Insights of this kind are ideas, and many of them deserve consideration of a sort. But none of them are any more appropriately imposed by fiat on the general public than would be a prohibition against consuming alcohol, or, more to the point, against abortion, or a requirement that one not mix milk and meat. These are matters of private choice.

The Elect are welcome to their private choices, such as forbidding interracial romance, discouraging black people from being specific, and teaching toddlers to think of themselves as members of races in an oppositional relationship. (Note that the Elect are indeed a sect, through and through!) But beyond their meetings, if the Elect are to insist on being an evangelist kind of religion, they must learn to try to spread their philosophy via civil and gradual suasion. The Pentecostal makes no converts knocking on people's doors and calling them Satanists. Or, if they did, we would know there was something they were scaring, rather than talking, people into.

The Elect object here that they are different because this is about racism, as if what they preach is self-evidently logical. But let's recall what they mean by that with a last look into what's in the little book they would be carrying if they knocked on your door:

1. When black people say you have insulted them, apologize with profound sincerity and guilt.	Don't put black people in a position where you expect them to forgive you. They have dealt with too much to be expected to.
2. Don't assume that all, or even most, black people like hip-hop, are good dancers, and so on. Black people are a conglomeration of disparate individuals. "Black culture" is code for "pathological, primitive ghetto people."	Don't expect black people to assimilate to "white" social norms, because black people have a culture of their own.
3. Silence about racism is violence.	Elevate the voices of the oppressed over your own.
4. You must strive eternally to understand the experiences of black people.	You can never understand what it is to be black, and if you think you do you're a racist.
5. Show interest in multiculturalism.	Do not culturally appropriate. What is not your culture is not for you, and you may not try it or do it.
6. Support black people in creating their own spaces and stay out of them.	Seek to have black friends. If you don't have any, you're a racist. And if you claim any, they'd better be *good* friends—albeit occupying their private spaces that you aren't allowed in.
7. When whites move away from black neighborhoods, it's white flight.	When whites move into black neighborhoods, it's gentrification, even when they pay black residents generously for their houses.

8. If you're white and date only white people, you're a racist.	If you're white and date a black person, you are, if only deep down, exotifying an "other."
9. Black people cannot be held accountable for everything every black person does.	All whites must acknowledge their personal complicitness in the perfidy of "whiteness" throughout history.
10. Black students must be admitted to schools via adjusted grade and test-score standards to ensure a representative number of them and foster a diversity of views in classrooms.	It is racist to assume a black student was admitted to a school via racial preferences, and racist to expect them to represent the "diverse" view in classroom discussions.

The above is church; it has no place in state.

Sample scripts.

If you need perspective, talk to anyone you know from a formerly Communist country. A great many of our immigrants from Russia and China are mystified at how readily so many smart Americans are rolling over in the face of rhetoric these immigrants recognize as what they escaped or what their own parents and relatives had their lives ruined by.

Or think of sharks. You can make a shark approaching you go away by bopping it on the nose. Something about that throws them and makes them turn around. We need to, metaphorically, start bopping Elects on the nose when they come for us.

I of course mean nothing physical and intend not the slightest dog whistle to that effect. The metaphor, though, is simply invaluable. The bop will be with words only, and will consist simply of telling them no. To be sure, these are sharks who, when they turn away, also call you a white supremacist on Twitter. But truly, life can be so much worse.

It would be worse, for example, to allow the threat of name-calling to usher benevolent bullies into taking over how we think, teach, dream, and live with their glowering punitive ideology. After a while, too, the sharks will start simply turning away without taking out their phones (okay, the analogy is now strained!) because they will realize that the name-calling doesn't get them what they want.

Sample exchanges:

"I don't think I'm a white supremacist, and you aren't
going to change my mind. Let's move on to a
different topic."
(And if the Elect leaves the gathering in disgust at
your heresy, let them; continue the gathering with
no staged confession of guilt, and do not apologize to
the Elect later when he writes you grousing that what
you said was "problematic," i.e. blasphemous.)

"I will not sign this petition, and I don't care what you
call me when I don't, on Twitter or anywhere else."

(Twitter mobs are hideous, but some of you could consider just laying low for a few weeks. Believe me, except in the most extreme cases, it passes and life goes on.)

"I will not retract [this innocent thing I said or wrote], and you can call me anything you want. And if you try to get me fired, I will push back and write about *you* on Twitter."
(And do it—you'll probably find you have more friends than you think. Social media brings people like you together as much as it does the Elect, and people like you are getting wearier by the week of the Elect's abusiveness.)

"This religion has no place in this school's curriculum. It is indeed a religion, because I'm afraid you don't seem able to explain your take on this issue with what I think of as logic. If *White Fragility* and *How to Be an Antiracist* do it for you, you don't seem to be able to tell me why, which suggests that those books are not as valuable as you seem to think. If you insist on exposing my children to this religion when they are supposed to be getting an education, I will gather a group of parents and we will transfer our children to another school. And we will write all about *you* on Twitter before, while, and after we do it."

(If this becomes a trend nationwide, it will become ever
easier to get other parents to join you publicly.)

"No, we will not refocus our entire curriculum around
antiracism. We do not think of battling racism as the
most important goal of our program; we think of it as
one among many, and we are proud of how we
were going about it before. We are open to some
suggestions as to how we could do better, but never
will antiracism be the main focus of our work here,
and if you don't like it, go try to take over another
department."
(And the social media storm would begin, along with
flyers posted, a scruffy protest in front of the
building, and such. Stick it out—as countless
perfectly sensible alumni and parents cheer you on, as
well as, albeit often discreetly, most of the rest of the
campus. We cannot let these little religious mobs
shape how we live.)

"You're telling me I'm a racist, but I am more committed
to actually helping poor people of color than you are."
(And look them in the eye and maintain your gaze,
without mumbling "I'm sorry." This has a way of
making a difference—don't look away; stand your
ground. I can guarantee you that on some level, your
interlocutor knows that, for example, fighting for

vocational training and the end of drug prohibition makes you a "realer" ally of black people than sitting in circles attesting to white privilege and apologizing about it as Rome burns.)

We must say no to these people, in quest of a result: An understanding will gradually coalesce among them that they need to step up their game, or, better, step it down. A communal realization will set in, after a while even explicitly acknowledged by its unofficial leaders, that shaming isn't working anymore. Again, yes, it can be hard to be called a racist even if you know you aren't one, just as we shudder at the thought of being called pedophiles or climate deniers or, hell, of having not quite gotten *Mad Men*.

But here we must see ourselves as engaging in a kind of valor. Mr. Solzhenitsyn, in *The Gulag Archipelago*, noted, in words sadly applicable to our time on this issue:

> We have gotten used to regarding as *valor* only valor in war (or the kind that's needed for flying in outer space), the kind which jingle-jangles with medals. We have forgotten another concept of *valor—civil valor*. And that's all our society needs, just that, just that, just that! That's all we need and that's exactly what we haven't got.

To be sure, what we process as valor the Elect will classify as a racist "backlash," further priding themselves on their righteousness in the face of it. But if, amid that righteousness, they gradually go back to 2010 and conduct themselves as one voice at the table out of many, our job is done. Social history is never perfect, and as long as the Elect's reign of terror is stanched, we are in a better place, regardless of whether they understand why.

Nota bene: Don't get sidetracked by that person on the other side of the dinner table who says that the Elect are not a real threat compared with overtly racist right-wing extremism. Revolutions are always "messy," one hears, with the implication that in the grand scheme of things, the Elect's current reign is just a matter of the left working out some kinks. Few people settling for this view would call the alt-right just "messy," and my simple answer is: Imagine the Elect mob coming after you.

If your emotion amid the "mess" of that would be terror, then it's a conclusive demonstration that this is something we need to pay serious attention to. Terror becomes a good thing neither when it comes from the left nor even when it comes from black people. Reason must prevail. This is the heart of the Enlightenment. The abolitionists knew it; Civil Rights leaders knew it; today's liberals know it. Only the Elect propose that rationality, where it discomfits them, is mere "whiteness."

It is neither progress nor messy for people to lose their jobs and reputations for not putting the overturning of power differentials at the very core of every single thing they ever do, express, or feel. It is neither progress nor messy for black people to be taught that our main value is not as individuals, but in how articulately we play victim in order to help whites feel good about themselves in feeling guilty about it. The Elect is not merely some mess. The Elect is a scourge and must be treated as such.

Be Spartacus.

It is natural to fear going up against the parishioners who so fervently disagree, with their ten-dollar words and artful sarcasm and air of surety. But I promise you: There is room in this society for speaking the truth and living to tell about it. I present a few examples fresh in my mind as I write:

Trader Joe's refused to pull its lines of products named, tongue-in-cheek, Trader José, Trader Ming's, and the like, in the face of a richly signed petition fostered by an Elect teenager thinking of herself sincerely as doing her job amid the racial reckoning of 2020. Trader Joe's said no and survives, while the teenager soon disappeared herself from social media.

Arkansas's Harding University refused to take the name of a former school president off of a building, despite that he initially opposed integrating the school in the 1960s. They based their decision on evaluating the man's entire life trajectory, which included changing his views about integration and doing extensive good works in Africa. This fit this Christian university's creed, which includes forgiveness, which its fellow Elect religion does not. The university lives on; its leaders said no and survived.

Princeton mathematician Sergiu Klainerman and classicist Joshua Katz publicly disavowed and critiqued the Princeton manifesto assailing the school as racist. They were respecting black people in doing so, and these professors, despite being roasted as you-know-whats on social media (and in Katz's case, subjected to a campus newspaper article unearthing embarrassing matters in his past), will not be selling pencils on the street anytime soon. They said no and survived.

University of California, Davis, mathematician Abigail Thompson similarly condemned the nature of a "diversity statement" foisted upon faculty at that school and stood down detractors. She said no and survived.

The Unitarian reverend Todd Eklof (see chapter 2), excommunicated for taking issue with Elect ideology, is pushing back, with the support of hundreds of his flock who have stood by him and many others who have left the church in protest. Reverend Eklof will survive.

More than a hundred established artists have petitioned against museums pulling their exhibits of the paintings of Philip Guston, many of which include figures of Klansmen intended as thought-provoking abstractions. The museums were afraid certain people would feel these images as "centering" reviled bigotry or "triggering" traumatic memory. But these artists understand that this was retrogressive, willfully feigning a blindness to how art works. Guston's work, and these artists, will survive.

Sandia National Laboratories employee Casey Petersen pushed back against the lab's Elect-style "diversity statement," including in a widely viewed YouTube video. He was widely reviled, but also supported by, for example, a black Sandia engineer. At this writing, he still has his job. He survived.

The president of Northwestern University, Morton Schapiro, granted some honesty to student protesters demanding the defunding of the campus police via hurling invective and defacing the sidewalk outside of his home: "This isn't actually speaking truth to power or furthering your cause. It is an abomination and you should be ashamed of yourselves." Of course, the usual suspects called him a racist and demanded his resignation. "I absolutely stand by exactly what I said," he insisted. And there he stands, as I write.

Pedro Domingos, professor of computer science and engineering at the University of Washington, questioned an Elect agenda requiring an "ethics test" for submissions to the flagship Conference on Artificial Intelligence and its associated publication. He was summarily attacked by a leading Elect practitioner in the field, complete with the usual summoning of troops, ad hominem accusations, and attempts to pillory even people who had liked him on social media. Domingos stood firm, watched temperate-minded colleagues gradually start speaking out in his favor, and is today alive and well to tell about it.

There are others whose names I should not yield, such as the academic in a position of authority who, commanded to tar certain persons as racist on Elect grounds, resigned from the post despite the salary cut that returning to mere faculty status entailed. This person has survived, as have so many others, and as so many others will.

THE ELECT WILL be ever convinced that if you join these brave, self-possessed survivors, you are, regardless of your color, a moral pervert in bed with white supremacy.

But you aren't, and you know it.

Stand up.

ACKNOWLEDGMENTS

This book frankly leapt out of me during the summer of 2020. My thanks go first to my agent Dan Conaway, who with grace and forbearance grappled with his client writing a book inconveniently hot on the heels of another one, and as time went by, expertly steered it into publication. Bria Sandford at Portfolio has been, also, a bracingly expert editor.

This is the first book I have written to which I owe such significant thanks to people I do not actually know. The thousands of missives I have received since the summer of 2020 from people as dismayed by the new influence of the Elect as I am have vastly enlightened me as to the nature and scope of the phenomenon, including furnishing me with countless examples from where they live. The volume of those missives has, and continues to, outstrip my ability to answer them individually. However, I have learned loads from all of them. Much of the Catechism of Contradictions in chapter 1 is inspired by someone who has contacted me about the issues in this book and who, because of the prosecutorial nature of the movement I am referring to, preferred to stay anonymous but knows who they are.

Of people I do know, Dan Akst, Aileen Kawabe, Joe Kolman, Lenore Skenazy, and Dan and Rose Subotnik have especially helped shape the thoughts that went into this book.

NOTES

CHAPTER 2: THE NEW RELIGION

32 **"He is a wonderful man universally loved by students":** Maria Lencki, "Northwestern Law Faculty Refuse to Explain Why They Introduced Themselves as Racists," *College Fix*, September 8, 2000, https://www.thecollegefix.com/northwestern-law-faculty-refuse-to-explain-why-they-introduced-themselves-as-racists.

41 **A black writer has objected:** Charlton McIlwain, "Racism Cannot be Reduced to Mere Computation," *Slate*, August 29, 2020.

42 **The erasure is as stunning as it is thorough:** Jonathan Holloway, "Isn't 400 Years Enough?" *New York Times*, February 10, 2021, https://www.nytimes.com/2021/02/10/opinion/black-history-month.html.

52 **Victims of this mental virus can be recognized:** Richard Trudeau, "UUs in the Pews, Please Help!" *Truly Open Minds and Hearts* (blog), June 24, 2020, https://trulyopenmindsandhearts.blog/2020/06/24/uus-in-the-pews-please help.

57 **A professor at the Steinhardt School at New York University:** From a confidential message to the author.

CHAPTER 3: WHAT ATTRACTS PEOPLE TO THIS RELIGION?

62 **The difference between good old-fashioned left and modern Elect:** Richard Delgado, *The Coming Race War?* (New York: New York University Press, 1996), p. 29.

62 **A new politics of identification:** Regina Austin, "'The Black Community,' Its Lawbreakers, and a Politics of Identification," *Southern California Law Review* 65, no. 4 (May 1992), pp. 1769–817.

65 **New York City school board meeting in 2020:** CEC District 2, "CEC D2 Working Business Meeting," YouTube video, 1:25:24, June 29, 2020, https://www.youtube.com/watch?v=VbJr2-55MVk&t=2541s.

67-68 Nick Srnicek and Alex Williams have called "folk politics": Nick Srnicek and Alex Williams, *Inventing the Future: Postcapitalism and a World Without Work* (London: Verso, 2015).

69 "People imbibe because they like it": Douglas Murray, *The Strange Death of Europe: Immigration, Identity, Islam* (London: Bloomsbury, 2017).

70 If you wish to expel religion: Sigmund Freud, *The Future of an Illusion* (New York: W. W. Norton, 1989).

79 Michael Lind is sadly accurate: Michael Lind, "What Politics Is(n't)," *Smart Set*, September 30, 2016, https://www.thesmartset.com/what-politics-isnt.

84 "I'm valid when I'm disrespected": N. R. Kleinfield, "Guarding the Borders of the Hip-Hop Nation," *New York Times,* July 6, 2000, https://www.nytimes.com/2000/07/06/us/guarding-the-borders-of-the-hip-hop-nation.html.

88 a black psychiatrist named Cobbs squares off against a white woman: Elizabeth Lasch-Quinn, *Race Experts* (Lanham, MD: Rowman & Littlefield, 2002), p. 100.

CHAPTER 4: WHAT'S WRONG WITH IT BEING A RELIGION?

98 Black boys get suspended and expelled from schools more than other kids: Christopher Paslay, *Exploring White Fragility* (Lanham, MD: Rowman & Littlefield, 2021).

110 "white empiricism" as keeping black women out of physics: Chandra Prescod-Weinstein, "Making Black Women Scientists under White Empiricism: The Racialization of Epistemology in Physics," *Signs* 45, no. 2 (January 2020), pp. 421–27.

CHAPTER 6: HOW DO WE WORK AROUND THEM?

166 I almost never attend casual faculty functions: Chris Lebron, "White America Wants Me to Conform. I Won't Do It," *New York Times,* June 16, 2020, https://www.nytimes.com/2020/06/16/opinion/black-academia-racism.html.

175 "To recognize something as a religion": Charles Fain Lehman, "Review: 'Strange Rites' by Tara Isabella Burton," *Washington Free Beacon,* June 14, 2020, https://freebeacon.com/culture/review-strange-rites-by-tara-isabella-burton/.

INDEX